CREATIVE GENIUS YOU

THE EQUATION THAT MAKES

YOU

GREAT!

BY PATTI D

DRAWINGS BY

Cover and Illustrations by Scott Ward.
Interior Design: J. L. Saloff
Print ISBN: 978-0-9839856-5-5
Ebook ISBN: 978-0-9839856-6-2
Library of Congress Control Number: 2022922043

CONTENTS

TO ALL OF THE ENTREPRENEURS AND CREATORS WHO GET UP EVERY MORNING AND TIRELESSLY WORK TO MAKE THE WORLD A BETTER PLACE. THIS ONE'S FOR YOU!

FOREWORD

I've always been fascinated by science and the scientific method. From Thomas Edison and his philosophy that there are no failures in invention (just ways to not solve the problem) to Albert Einstein and his unique perspectives on reality ... and a host of other brilliant people who have sought to express our world in an understandable way — they have all inspired me in one way or another.

The human equation, of course, is not as simple as calculating the volume of a sphere, say, but if we can find a way to understand our own creativity and, through that, create a future for ourselves and for others that sets the world alight, something truly magical can happen.

And that's what you'll find in this book.

I've known Patti for a number of years. We've shared stages together, working with organisations around the world, featured on one another's podcasts and I've even been coached by her. She's an expert at helping people create a clear vision of the future they want to have and take the bold steps needed to get there.

Over the years I've seen her use a range of techniques and strategies to bring that future vision to life in creative and ingenious ways. It was Patti who showed me how being a genius isn't limited to a select few, but is something within us all. And it was because of Patti that I started to draw pictures of my own future — every single morning — to keep me moving steadily in the right direction.

It isn't always easy to trust your creativity and believe in your own genius, especially in a world that seems to roll from crisis to crisis, but **CREATIVE GENIUS YOU** is alive and well in every single one of us and I firmly believe that we all have the ability to bring it out to create a fantastic future.

So, even if math wasn't your favourite subject in school, you will find that the **CREATIVE GENIUS EQUATION** is going to give you an insight into your inner power and talent. In doing so it will unlock the future that you have long suspected was there for you but never dared to do more than dream about.

This is going to be amazing!

Pete Cohen, July 2022

PREFACE

Equations fascinate me. As a freshman in high school, when I showed a real flair for working with math equations, my advisor suggested I transfer into an accelerated pre-calculus class. Excited, I arrived in class to find the teacher (a belt cinched snugly just above his bulging belly in the most distracting manner) apparently in a race to explain abstract concepts as quickly as possible, never pausing to note whether anyone, including me, his newest bewildered student, could follow along. I jumped in, doing my best to decode what he was saying. After all, my love of equations was why I was there, along with the fact that I secretly thought of myself as a bit of a math genius.

I did my best, but I was not making much progress, so I asked my dad, the smartest guy I knew, for help. After an hour of head-scratching, he too gave up in frustration. I struggled through the rest of the semester, barely made a passing grade, and never ventured into the world of advanced mathematics again.

It wasn't until years later, as I began to use images to help others understand and incorporate abstract ideas that it occurred to me; if my math teacher had used simple pictures to illustrate complex math concepts, the other students and I may have understood calculus. Instead, my inability to grasp what he was **TELLING** me, not **SHOWING** me, gave birth to the belief that I simply wasn't smart enough for advanced mathematics.

Later, I got involved in putting together the school yearbook. I loved writing and photography! Design fascinated me and I became absorbed in the challenge of translating the experiences of our high school community into visual images. I learned about the concepts of good visual design, and in the process, I became intrigued by the power of graphic imagery to convey complex abstract ideas — a process that is profoundly satisfying to both the person creating the images and those who view them.

A seed was planted in me from what I learned about the power images have to embody dreams, visions and ideas; and in turn, the impact images can have on the person viewing them. This understanding is at the core of my development of the **CREATIVE GENIUS EQUATION** process. I know that if you can tap into your own creativity to visualize and draw what you hope for, the chances increase significantly that you will bring them into being.

The **CREATIVE GENIUS EQUATION** is an intuitive process that most people find easy to grasp and apply in their lives. In fact, as you learn more, you'll probably find that you are already using some form of this process each time you identify a goal and work to achieve it. Using the tools described in this book you'll engage both the intuitive parts of your subconscious mind and the more pragmatic, linear parts of your conscious mind. Together they make it possible for you to access your own innate, boundless creativity to set in motion the future you desire.

I have been holding the mantle of the **CREATIVE GENIUS EQUATION** for many years, using it to work with others and studying its interplay in the fields of collaboration and change. Now, in a time when all of us need as many tools as we can find to navigate the speed of change we face, I want to pass the baton to you, so that you can expand your use of the equation's elements and create your own roadmap for any change you are facing. Take what sounds fun and try it, evolve it and be sure to let me know what you discover so I can pass it on to others.

Put a blank piece of paper in front of you and give yourself permission to draw what you imagine could be the reality for your future self and the flow of creativity and genius can be unbelievable. When given the freedom to take a concept and expand it, you can tap into a pool of new ideas just waiting for you.

My goal in writing this book is to provide your inner Creative Genius with simple tools to help you listen and trust that powerful hard-wired talent whenever you need or want to.

YOU ARE THE CREATIVE GENIUS EQUATION IN ACTION.

WELCOME TO CREATIVE GENIUS YOU.

INTRODUCTION

As a keynote speaker, I sometimes greet my audience with, "**HELLO, CREATIVE GENIUSES!**"

This usually elicits looks of confusion and it takes a few seconds before they grasp the fact that, yes, I am talking to them. If I ask, "**HOW MANY OF YOU THINK OF YOURSELF AS A CREATIVE GENIUS?**" a few people will tentatively raise their hands, sheepishly looking around as if embarrassed. Why? Because the term "**CREATIVE GENIUS**" is one we tend to associate with someone who has made it as an acclaimed artist or perhaps as a wildly successful innovative business owner. The underlying assumption is that to be a Creative Genius you must be larger than life, someone capable of brilliant, life-changing ideas that meet our culture's definition of success.

I have a different definition for the term **CREATIVE GENIUS**. While you may be willing to admit that some part of what you do every day is creative, I'd guess that you might still hesitate to see yourself as a genius. But what if the mere act of moving through your day, navigating problems and finding solutions is proof that you are uniquely creative and indicates your genius? I believe what many of us what we're missing is our ability to recognize and nourish the Creative Genius within ourselves.

Any time you solve a problem, big or small, you are drawing on creativity to calculate possible outcomes and envision possible solutions. When faced with a problem, the synapses in your brain begin to fire at lightning speed, sorting through past experiences stored as visual memories in the part of your brain called the hippocampus. Within seconds the images are shared with your prefrontal cortex, the part of your brain responsible for problem-solving. All options are weighed and explored. In a flash, your brain ranks them and finally selects the solution that seems to best solve the problem. All of this happens in seconds without much effort on our part. This process of creative problem solving is part of our neurological wiring. The challenge is to learn how to consciously tap into it whenever we need it.

It may surprise you that one of the first steps towards activating your Creative Genius is to use your imagination network or the part of your brain that uses daydreams to imagine possible outcomes. In fact, you're doing it right now as you read this page. To understand

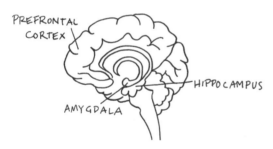

what you are reading your brain automatically transforms these words into a sequence of pictures that allows you to create a story and understand the concepts I'm describing. But because imagination isn't tactile or tangible (**MEANING YOU CAN'T HOLD IT IN YOUR HANDS**) most people don't value this simple act of creative imagining as a serious approach to problem solving.

Creativity is an integral part of each of us, not something that some lucky people have while others don't. It's a natural ability that is hardwired into your brain. Knowing how and when to consciously access creativity and then making the choice to apply it, is what makes the difference. In this book you will learn simple, yet powerful steps you can take to expand your ability to engage imagination and enrich every aspect of your life.

If most of us struggle to grasp the fact that we are creative, consider the issues that arise when we encounter the label "genius"! Where did we get the idea that only a select few qualify to be geniuses?

The word genius itself comes from the Latin word, **INGENIUM**, meaning "**OF YOUR INNATE TALENTS AND CAPABILITIES.**" This concept is more in line with what I am proposing. We all have

a genius for something — things we do with little effort. These acts may not garner widespread acclaim, vast amounts of wealth or any notice at all. They are just things we do as an authentic expression of who we are and what we care about. So, keep in mind when I use the word genius, I am not limiting it to someone like Einstein. This is not about high IQ — it's much, much more than that.

Genius can be as simple as figuring out how to fix the kitchen door, or it can be as complicated as finding a cure for malaria. All of us are swimming in a sea of potential genius all day, every day. This wealth of genius, combined with a spark of creativity, is responsible for every decision we make. I think it is time we redefine genius as the innate ability to generate ideas and imagination to envision what is possible and claim it.

In my Creative Genius sessions with organizations, work teams and entrepreneurs, their visions and goals inspire me to draw pictures that begin to take shape as a map. When complete, the map serves as a visual guide, outlining their goals and achievement. Over the twenty-five years that I have done this work, I have seen Creative Genius everywhere, in every meeting or conversation that occurs.

Once, as I prepared to conduct a Creative Genius drawing session with a group of bank employees, their CEO told them,

> "EACH OF YOU NEEDS TO TAKE ARTISTIC CONTROL OF YOUR SKILLS. DEFINE AND REFINE WHAT YOU DO BEST AND USE IT TO HELP THE COMPANY PROVIDE EXTRAORDINARY SERVICE TO OUR CUSTOMERS. I WILL TRUST YOU TO SERVE THEM, DOING WHAT YOU DO BEST, BY BRINGING YOUR CREATIVITY WITH YOU TO WORK EVERY DAY."

She both challenged and inspired them to integrate their innate creativity by trusting their ideas. Her words perfectly set the stage for their session with me.

But it was a rare moment. I think I can safely say that bank employees are seldom encouraged to be creative! The CEO urged them to refine their creative skills and begin to find new ways to meet challenges. Even more remarkable, she promised to support them when they did.

If you are an organization leader or a small business owner, how often do you ask your team to tap into their Creative Genius? In the business world, the quest for bigger, more profitable solutions and emphasis on the bottom line are priorities. As a result, competition between employees to achieve these goals becomes the measure of success. Yet research shows that to truly succeed in the business world, work teams need to align their projects with their talents and strengths first because this leads to greater returns.

The secret I am sharing with you is this: one of the best ways to get results is to create an environment where you and your employees are encouraged to actively cultivate a relationship with your Creative Genius. This connection not only opens the floodgates, allowing new ideas and solutions to become clear but, more importantly, it gives everyone a sense of satisfaction and accomplishment. It validates their inner knowing and often aligns with their life purpose. The result is a work environment that fosters innovation and provides incentive for everyone to stay engaged.

Consider this book a challenge to those of you who would never in a million years think of yourself as either Creative or a Genius, and encouragement to those of you who already do. As the CEO of your own life, give yourself permission to listen more deeply to your own creative voice and then get the support you need to act on your insights.

Whether you hope to bring more creativity into your personal life, seek better health, financial security or just experience happiness and contentment, the **CREATIVE GENIUS EQUATION** is an essential tool that can help you reach those goals. If you practice the techniques I am sharing with you, you will increase your ability to use your inherent strength and talent. That will allow you to create better solutions which give you the changes you desire.

I BELIEVE IN THE POWER
OF CREATIVE GENIUS YOU
AND GUARANTEE
THAT IF YOU
SINCERELY IMPLEMENT
THE METHODS DESCRIBED IN THIS BOOK
AND YOU DON'T EXPERIENCE
POSITIVE WORK OR LIFE CHANGES,

I'LL GIVE YOU YOUR MONEY BACK.

1. THE INNER DRIVE TO EXPAND

Just out of college, I worked as an artist-in-residence, teaching theatre in schools. Students at most of the schools I worked in had never met an artist, let alone had an artist of any kind in their classroom. It was an exhilarating and challenging experience for an actor with little teaching experience, but things started off well. The kids liked what I was doing and teachers and parents were impressed with the stories and performances the students gave after just one week of Acting 101.

Buoyed by my successes I accepted a brief artist-in-residence job at a school district in rural Idaho.

The first week at one of the schools went like clockwork. Students wrote and performed short plays with some of the teachers joining in. The teaching staff was thrilled to have an artist-in-residence working with the students. In my second week, I went on to share my genius with another school, patting myself on the back for how well it was going. Unfortunately, I had forgotten that. . .

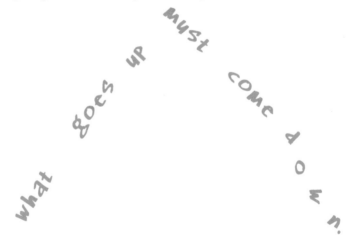

what goes up must come down.

In my final class of the first day with a group of fifth graders, as a closing exercise, I divided them into two lines facing each other from opposite sides of the room. I'd used this activity before to generate some laughs and leave them energized for the next day. Then, after many rounds of touching knees and toes, out of my mouth comes, **"RUN UP TO YOUR PARTNER, KISS THEM AND RUN BACK!"**

Usually kids this age rebel. No one kisses anyone, everyone says, **"YUCK"** or something along those lines and we all have a good laugh. Just in case they think I am serious I quickly yell, **"JUST KIDDING! GREAT WORK, THANK YOU AND SEE YOU TOMORROW!"**

I start packing up my things and the voice inside my head is congratulating me for another successful day.

What I hadn't noticed was that two girls had run up to each other, covered their mouths with their hands and pretended to kiss. Now this was during the 1980s, in a very conservative rural community, so you can imagine that this kind of joking around was not considered funny by **EVERYONE**.

The next morning, I passed a group of parents huddled outside the principal's office. I wave a cheery hello only to be met with a full-on group **STINK-EYE**. It seems they had called for a meeting with the principal to complain about me. Some of the kids had gone home and told their parents the story about the kissing incident. These parents were accusing me of attempting to bring homosexuality into the classrooms and they wanted me out! During first period, I was called into the office to meet with the principal to straighten things out.

In the 1980s, the AIDS epidemic was on the rise. Misinformation and fear created an environment where hate crimes were common, especially in rural areas. Many of the social and legal changes that have made this kind of bigotry unacceptable were still many years away. As an outsider who looked, talked and dressed differently, I was suspect and absolutely no one in the community, **INCLUDING THE PRINCIPAL**, had my back. The situation was dangerous, and I felt scared and vulnerable.

I was told to continue with my classes while they decided what to do. All the confidence I had at the start of the week disappeared instantly, and I seriously considered packing my bags and leaving.

After school I couldn't wait to get back to where I was staying — a dreary rental house furnished with a mattress on the floor, one chair, a small table and a kitchen equipped with a few battered pots and pans. I have always wondered who decided this would be a great place for the artist-in-residence, but perhaps it was an omen.

While dining on my instant ramen, I sank into a deep state of shame and despair. As a gay woman, I knew the potential for danger to me personally was real. My attempt at a joke had ignited a huge community controversy, putting me right at the center. Even though the parents and teachers really knew nothing about my personal life, they knew that I was different from them, and they weren't sure I was going to play by their rules.

I called my boss, the state coordinator of the artist-in-residence program and, while she was supportive, she told me I had two options:

I could leave the program and go home, or I could stay and help the town (and myself) learn and grow. Even with her support, I was faced with two choices, neither of which I liked. **I FELT COMPLETELY ALONE**.

I remember going outside to stare at the night sky looking for a sign that would help me decide what to do. I had recently started meditating and exploring my spirituality so, in my despair, I decided to meditate. I hoped this might give me some insight into what my next step should be. At the very least, I hoped I might be able to calm down and think more clearly.

Sitting cross-legged on the bare floor of my so-called bedroom, I closed my eyes and began to move into a meditative state. After a few minutes of breathing deeply, I decided to try a visualization I'd read about.

In this visualization you imagine being outside of your body looking back at yourself. I'd tried this visualization before without any notice-able results but, on this day, in my state of emotional rawness, an amazing thing happened. My whole body started to shake uncontrollably. I heard a loud whooshing sound and felt a brilliant white light fill my whole being. I can only describe this as feeling like I had exploded into a million pieces. I felt myself merge with the universe and was instantly filled with a sense of ecstatic connection to everything and everybody. I suddenly saw that we are all connected, and **WE ARE ALL LOVE**.

Then, as quickly as it began, it was over. I sat there for a long time filled with awe and joy, and deeply at peace.

Clearly there were many things I knew nothing about, including how such a dramatic shift in my own awareness could have the power to change my perception of self and other. I wasn't sure who I could talk to about what I'd experienced but it gave me the strength to go back to school the next day knowing that I was exactly where I was supposed to be, with the courage to face whatever happened next.

Now, looking back at that time in my life, I can see that what I'd done was tap into my Creative Genius; the source that guides me in the

right direction. In class that day and every day afterwards, I was energized by my meditation experience. I found I had the strength to stay and face that small town community. Inwardly, I knew and trusted that everything would be okay and that I would be okay too.

In Saul Bellow's spectacular Nobel Prize acceptance speech he said. . .

ONLY ART PENETRATES
THE SEEMING REALITIES OF
THIS WORLD.
THERE IS ANOTHER REALITY,
THE GENUINE ONE,
WHICH WE LOSE SIGHT OF.
THIS OTHER REALITY
IS ALWAYS SENDING US HINTS
WHICH, WITHOUT ART,
WE CAN'T RECEIVE.

SAUL BELLOW

As I arrived at my classroom from then on, I took up the mantle of myself as an artist in a strange and foreign community. I accepted that it was my job to shake things up a bit and show others how to trust their instincts, tell their stories and honor their choices. As the artist-in-residence, I was committed to showing students, teachers, administrators and their families that when you access and express your creativity, you connect with your own Creative Genius, learning more about yourself and the world around you than you could ever imagine.

MY RENEWED COMMITMENT AND DETERMINATION PAID OFF. In the end, the student's performances were magnificent, and their parents were proud and perhaps even surprised. The principal invited me to extend my stay to run a 5k race along with the students, parents and teachers to raise funds for their arts program. When I crossed the finish line, I placed first in my age category and, as the principal gave me my medal, he made a short speech expressing the school's gratitude for my work with the students.

This experience was a turning point for me. It fueled my desire to embrace and partner with my Creative Genius and see this as a way to build my confidence when faced with tough challenges. I had tapped into a source of wisdom that could guide me through the roughest of waters.

I imagine that **YOU ALSO** feel a burning desire to grow, learn, explore, and better understand yourself and your experiences. When you look at the path that led to where you are today, you can probably identify key turning points in your own journey. Challenging situations force us to dig deep for the courage and tenacity needed to keep going. You may have stepped up to learn a new skill or love someone more deeply, to lead your team or practice a sport until you had mastered it.

Whatever the turning points you faced, at some point you realized that you had to commit to solve the problem yourself. You had to roll up your sleeves and get your hands dirty because life wasn't going to move in to help you, unless you did your part.

That commitment is essential. William Hutchinson Murray, the Scottish mountaineer and writer said it simply, "**NOTHING HAPPENS UNTIL YOU DECIDE**." As with my experience, what got you here won't get you there. To step into the future you truly desire, **YOU TOO** need to take up the mantle of your Creative Genius to bring your fullest self to everything you do.

The connection you build with your Creative Genius will help you tap into this same knowingness to problem-solve and navigate inevitable obstacles. When you choose to take on bigger risks and go for the gold, you can build on your confidence.

Confidence being a product of prior performance, each successful step you take will rewire and build new neural pathways in your brain.

The quest to know **CREATIVE GENIUS YOU** is both inspiring and uncomfortable. As you step out of your comfort zone you will step onto the path towards the life you have longed for. Remind yourself as often as you can that what at first feels like an insurmountable obstacle, is in fact a select and powerful opportunity to strengthen your connection to your own innate and always accessible Creative Genius.

THE CREATIVE GENIUS EQUATION — THE SUBTLE MATH BEHIND GOAL ACHIEVEMENT

Your brain is designed to solve problems and find solutions. It is constantly processing incoming information and determining strategies for how to proceed. Here's how that works.

When you encounter a situation that appears to be a challenge, your brain's amygdala sends out alert signals so it can shift into problem-solving mode. It sorts through the records that have been housed in your hippocampus, through the memory-bank of experiences — everything you've seen, watched or done that relates to your current situation. Working at warp speed, it retrieves the memory slides or short movies and sends them to the prefrontal cortex.

Here everything is sorted and combined, like the eye doctor who asks you **"BETTER OR WORSE?"** **"THIS ONE OR THAT?"** Because

your prefrontal cortex can only handle a few images or ideas at a time, it deletes the ones that aren't useful. From the sequence of images, it finds the best of the best to help you deal with what's in front of you. Then your mind starts to daydream, playing out the scenario from different perspectives. **"WHAT IF YOU DID IT THIS WAY? OR SHOULD YOU DO IT THAT WAY?"** Finally, the mind will choose one avenue, the "**AHA**" moment comes and **BOOM!** You have your solution! "**I'M DOING THIS!**"

From there you step into action, doing whatever you now believe will resolve the situation. If all goes according to plan, the result is **FAIT ACCOMPLIS** or, at the very least, you up your insight and charge forward with your next step.

Problem solving is your brain's automated response, a sequence of pattern completion. Unfortunately, your first response when confronted with a problem is often a routine reaction, with your brain following established neural pathways. You tap into familiar ideas, connections and already applied solutions, to generate a response. This is kind of like giving a pat answer to someone's question.

YOUR BRAIN
CONSISTS OF
BILLIONS OF NEURONS
IN DIFFERENT REGIONS
THAT USE ELECTRICITY
TO COMMUNICATE
WITH ONE ANOTHER.
WHEN YOUR SYNAPSES
ARE FIRING IN SYNCHRONY,
THEY CREATE
UNIFIED COMBINATIONS
OF MILLIONS OF NEURONS
MARCHING IN LOCKSTEP
AS A HARMONIZED
"NEURAL NETWORK"
THAT IS LINKED TO
A SPECIFIC STATE
OF CONSCIOUSNESS,
YOUR THOUGHTS,
AND YOUR MOOD.

CHRISTOPHER BERGLAND,
THE ATHLETE'S WAY

When you consciously invoke your Creative Genius, however, using what I have coined the **CREATIVE GENIUS EQUATION**, the process changes. By pressing on new neural "levers" you interrupt your routine response and begin to explore and discover new ideas and possible solutions.

In 1992, I created a visual goal setting process called, **THE SNAPSHOT OF THE BIG PICTURE** which I later evolved into **DRAW YOUR FUTURE**® and began working with organizations and individuals to use it to achieve their goals. The essence of the process is that an individual or team will write words and draw pictures that depict where they feel they are right now (the current state), where they want to be a year, two years, ten years from now (the desired new reality), and then identify the **3 BOLD STEPS** they can take to get there (actions).

Early studies we did with the pharmaceutical company Hoffman LaRoche showed that, before using visual images to depict the future, only 36% of the people in their pharmaceutical division understood the company's vision and strategy. After using visual imagery, 94% of them understood the strategy and 84% of them said they understood how their work contributed to both the vision and the strategy. This kind of success rate when using visual imagery was repeated with other companies I worked with. It really seemed to work well.

But when the same process was used with individuals, the results varied. Some individuals didn't have the same immediate ability to achieve success, while others reported that, even when they hadn't thought about the picture after their initial drawing, when they looked back anywhere from one month to years later, everything in their desired new reality side of the map had happened.

The people who use **THE SNAPSHOT OF THE BIG PICTURE** process have often learned about it by watching my 2012 TEDx Rainier **DRAW YOUR FUTURE®** talk. They would copy or download the Big Picture template, create images depicting their current and desired states, and then identify the **3 BOLD STEPS** to get there.

The talk had reached a large audience, about 900,000 through the regular TEDx YouTube channel and about 6 million when it was posted on a renegade channel. Many of the viewers posted comments about their experience with the process I described.

I noticed that, similar to the Hoffman LaRoche study, about 75% of the comments indicated that even when the viewers followed my direction for drawing their own maps, their success using the process varied as well. This fascinated me and made me curious to find out how the process could be altered to achieve greater success for people.

I WANTED TO KNOW WHY: WHY, WHEN WE ARE INNATELY WIRED FOR CHANGE, AND TAKE ACTION TO CHANGE, DO WE GET STUCK?

I knew I had struggled with the process myself even though I had diligently followed all the steps. In 1995, I was working as a consultant, but I wanted to attract more work as a motivational speaker. While I had had some success, it felt like I was climbing a very steep mountain as I tried to get business from companies that booked speakers like me.

I wondered: was there a way I could accelerate my own success? Was there a systematic process I could apply for a shortcut to my goals?

I'd seen many clients accelerate their success using the **DRAW YOUR FUTURE**® process to set and achieve goals. But how was the visual imagery responsible for what was happening?

When we'd used the **DRAW YOUR FUTURE**® process, they would take the map I'd drawn and use it as a guide, applying their knowledge, experience and intuition to decide which of the things in their future they wanted to act on. With dedicated passion, they put their heads down and got to work on their goals.

As they achieved some success, they continued to repeat and iterate the process. Paying attention at each step, they found new ways to break through their challenges to access their own Creative Genius for even greater results, until they ticked off their goals one by one.

While it was clear that drawing a picture and using it as a map to guide their efforts was important, I began to look at what happened next. What were they doing to achieve their goals? What was happening after our initial mapping session? Was there an equation inherent in the process that led them to greater success?

THESE WERE THE COMPONENTS OF THE EQUATION THAT REPEATEDLY EMERGED

All the components of this equation seemed to be needed not only to set a goal, but also reach it. I named this iterative process The **CREATIVE GENIUS EQUATION**. It's a simple, elegant system that anyone can apply to achieve results, often beyond their wildest dreams!

When consciously used, it will connect your drive to do and be better, with your innately hardwired ability to problem solve. Each step in the process is a lever that you can press, push or stomp on to generate breakthroughs to challenges you may be facing in your business, team, health, career, or personal and professional relationships.

QUICK RECAP BEFORE WE GO INTO DETAIL

1. Creative Genius has been perceived, **WRONGLY**, as the domain of a few individuals and has outlived its previous definitions.

2. Creative Genius is an **INNATE, ACCESSIBLE PART** of you, that you can tap into to help you brainstorm and problem solve.

3. **DRAWINGS AND VISUAL IMAGERY** enhance how we process and remember information.

4. Results come from wherever **YOU PUT YOUR ATTENTION**. So, to have success in any field, you need to give it your attention.

5. **ANYONE** can accelerate their success using the **DRAW YOUR FUTURE®** process.

6. This book explores the **CREATIVE GENIUS EQUATION** — Imagination x Intuition + Desire x Drive = Outcome∞ (outcome to the infinite power).

EXERCISE: DRAW YOUR FUTURE®

Grab your journal or a few pieces of paper and a pen. If you prefer you can download the template here (or draw it yourself):

http://www.upyourcreativegenius.com/store

1. On one piece of paper, doodle around the edges to warm yourself up. Most of us have forgotten how to draw, so you want to rekindle it. Every time you do, hold your paper out, look at what you have drawn and say out loud, "**THAT'S FANTASTIC!**" This will help rewire your brain and banish the critic.

DRAW THE FOLLOWING SHAPES:

NOW TURN THOSE SHAPES INTO OBJECTS.

Remember, "**THAT'S FANTASTIC!**"

2. Now reflect on your current reality. Take a fresh piece of paper and, on the left side, capture in words and pictures what it feels like to be you right now. You can choose to reflect on just your business, just your personal life, a specific project or your whole life; it's your choice. Capture what's going well and what is challenging. Try to scatter your ideas around the area. **DON'T MAKE A LIST**. List-making activates the rational left hemisphere of the brain and we want to tap into a little disorganization and free-dom here. For the challenging aspects of life, consider that everything, without exception, is here to help you grow and learn. So, ask yourself, **WHAT SUPERPOWER IS THIS CHALLENGE HELPING ME TO GROW?** Then note that superpower by the challenge.

3. Take a short break to get some water or jump up and down.

4. When you sit down, imagine it is 1 year from today and you are exactly where you want to be. On the right side of the picture capture 4–5 ways you would like to feel on that day. You might feel more creative or abundant, or

you might feel more confident, or maybe something else. Scatter those words on the right side. Then add some specifics about the kinds of people you will meet, the business growth you will see, any aspects of your future you want to have. **CAPTURE IT IN WORDS AND PICTURES**.

5. Sit back and look at the current and desired future ("**THAT'S FANTASTIC**"). Then close your eyes and ask your Creative Genius — the part that knows all and is connected to your imagination and intuition — what are the 3 boldest things I can do to get myself from here to there? Draw three arrows from your current reality to your desired future and write each bold step in one of the arrows.

   Turn the page to see a sample map and a blank map for you to use, or download a map on my website:

   WWW.UPYOURCREATIVEGENIUS.COM

6. Check in with that drawing every day — Add to it as ideas strike you. Redraw it from time to time as the **CREATIVE GENIUS EQUATION** goes to work for you.

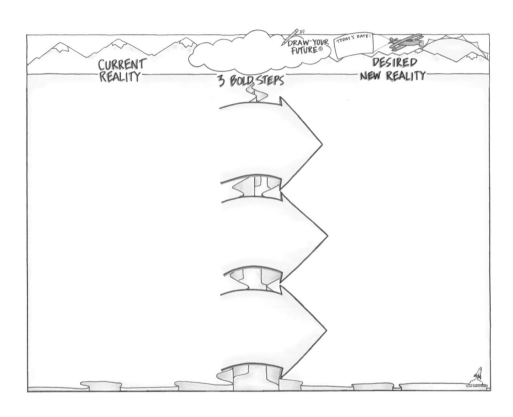

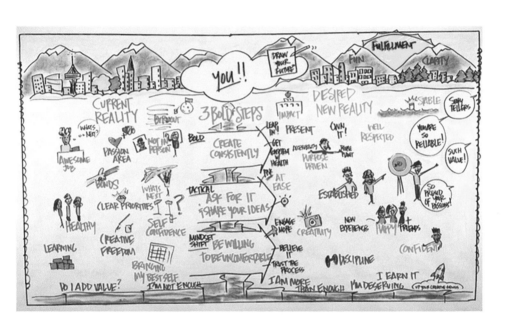

THE
CREATIVE
GENIUS
EQUATION

2. IMAGINATION

Do you remember having **IMAGINARY FRIENDS** when you were young? Most of us spent a great deal of our time as children creating entire imaginary worlds by ourselves or with other playmates. When you were young, you did this effortlessly and with great conviction. As you grew older, however, you probably engaged with your imagination less and less. I'll bet you were probably even told that daydreaming was a waste of time.

JUST ASKING
OR HEARING A QUESTION
PHRASED A CERTAIN WAY
PRODUCES AN ALMOST
PALPABLE FEELING
OF DISCOVERY
AND NEW UNDERSTANDING.
QUESTIONS PRODUCE
THE LIGHT BULB EFFECT.

WARREN BERGER,
A MORE BEAUTIFUL QUESTION

So maybe you aren't still having tea parties with your invisible friend Becca these days, but **YOUR IMAGINATION IS STILL AT WORK** — even if you think you never use it.

Consider the inner dialogue that runs in your head every waking minute. **WHO IS THAT VOICE TALKING TO?** And who is listening? Who is watching those daydreams you're creating as you imagine what you'll do next? If you sat down and thought about it, you'd realize that it's you, constantly playing out possible scenarios in your head and creating a myriad of outcomes.

Think about this scenario: You are running late for an appointment and, while waiting for traffic to move, you imagine how you will explain your delay, trying on different ways of getting you out of the jam the traffic has created.

YOU ARE ALSO CREATING THAT SCENARIO OF "STUCK IN TRAFFIC" IN YOUR HEAD RIGHT NOW AS YOU READ ABOUT IT!

You are **CONSTANTLY** creating scenarios for how to handle situations looming in the future, even mundane things like how you plan to spend your evening when you return home:

"LET'S SEE, SHOULD I TAKE A HOT BATH? NO, MAYBE A LONG WALK? BETTER YET, I'LL FLOP ON THE COUCH AND WATCH A NETFLIX SERIES!" YOU GET THE IDEA!

We all have an inner "daydream designer" who is constantly whipping up possibilities for dealing with every situation you get yourself into. Like a highly trained first responder, it's first on the scene to play out the drama of how things could go. Unfortunately, your daydream designer may automate to your inbred negative bias — that tendency to see the negative, to generate fear and a sense of hopelessness, so you will choose a more "safe" path. Negative bias often takes you down a well-worn path of things you have always thought or done and it's the first place you want to reroute your brain to instead tap into **CREATIVE GENIUS YOU.**

THE IMAGINATION NETWORK is involved in constructing dynamic image simulations based on personal past experiences. You use it during remembering, thinking about the future, and generally when imagining alternative perspectives and scenarios to the present.

The Imagination Network also helps you with social cognition. For instance, when you are imagining what someone else is thinking, this network is alive and active. What's cool about your Imagination Network is **WHEN YOU INTERRUPT YOUR AUTOMATED NEGATIVE BIAS**, you can tap into the creative aspect of your imagination for a more positive, forward moving solution.

Sometimes your negative bias may be what you believe about your ability to imagine. In many of the groups I work with, there are inevitably one or two people who will tell me that they don't think they have any imagination at all. It generally means that they have linked using their imagination with creativity, or that someone **TOLD** them early on that they had no imagination.

If you consider that you use your imagination every time you solve a problem, for example figuring out how to get home when the car breaks down (or any other routine challenge in your daily life) you can reframe your understanding of imagination. So when you hear yourself saying, "**I CAN'T COME UP WITH ANYTHING NEW OR ORIGINAL**," remember that's just your negative bias creeping in and there are simple tips to reroute that old belief to unleash your imagination.

The easiest way to activate your imagination is to ask yourself a question. **CURIOSITY IS THE MAGIC KEY** that unlocks new ideas and helps you sidestep negative thoughts. By asking a question about what you are looking at or challenged by, your brain starts randomly associating ideas and mixing them together to help you find new patterns. As you put together old ideas with new, you will often uncover a breakthrough thought or idea. Once this new idea pattern is created, your brain has a fresh place to start. Your prefrontal cortex cranks up and away you go!

As powerful as questions are for starting this, I have found that the entire process accelerates when you also draw a picture of the problem you are working on. Drawing an image helps you sort out the influences putting pressure on the situation and adds in all of the elements that you are holding in your mind. You can advance this by asking yourself questions like, "**WHAT RESULT WOULD THIS SOLUTION BRING? WHAT IF I TRIED THAT?**"

Even allowing yourself to mock-up outrageous or scary scenarios will stimulate amazing ideas. Try asking yourself, "**WHAT IDEA COULD I TRY THAT WOULD GET ME FIRED OR JAILED?**" Forcing yourself out of the norm also forces you outside of your comfort zone. As if you touched a lit match to kindling, you create the spark and kaboom to propel you into the unknown. Now you have open access to things you may have seen, heard or experienced, but weren't consciously thinking about, you step through a portal to find unique solutions.

"**DESIGN THINKING**" is a process that many companies use to develop customer solutions. If you aren't familiar with design thinking, the process is about identifying and clarifying the problem you are trying to solve as a first step, then understanding your potential customer. You create an "EMPATHY MAP" where you brainstorm who they are, what they feel, say, think or do and draw a picture of them or find pictures of their customer characteristics. Then you brainstorm ideas on how to solve that potential customer's problem.

Every step of design thinking forces you to use your imagination. It's a fluid and innate language we all possess. In fact, imagination is the one language we share as humans. It's on 24/7 and when you consciously harness its power, and direct it towards any problem you want to solve or vision you want to have, you'll see a dramatic shift in your ability to birth new ideas and increase your imagination quotient.

SETTING YOUR IMAGINATION FREE

Here is an example of how I tapped into a team's imagination to help them out of a rut. A corporate vice-president wanted to expand the potential of her team so they would be better problem solvers and decision makers. She was tired of having every small decision go through her.

I set up a game to build a team charter as an agreed set of behaviors to see exactly what happened when her team was faced with a decision. I wanted to see if there was an intervention point in the dynamics that resulted in their inability to find their own solutions.

The room was staged just like a board game, with big colored squares on the floor representing the different steps they normally followed in decision making. Then I added a bunch of blank squares to the game board. I gave the instructions that if someone landed on one of the random blank squares, they had the power to change anything about the process they were working on. They could change the people, place, roles, handoffs, or any part of the team dynamics they wanted. Game play ensued.

Delighted at the freedom this square gave them, it became everyone's favorite square. When someone landed on it, suddenly the person would take charge, confidently making big changes and moving everything around to new places on the board. They let go of the story that they had to run everything past the vice-president.

After a few hours, we stopped to reflect on what they had experienced. I asked what had made that random square so exciting and powerful?

"IT WAS LIKE A PORTAL TO MY UNCONSCIOUS AND MY IMAGINATION," ONE PERSON EXPLAINED. "IT GAVE ME PERMISSION TO DREAM UP THE IMPOSSIBLE AND ALLOWED ME TO BE FULLY RESPONSIBLE FOR MAKING MY OWN DECISIONS."

The concept was so powerful for them, **THEY TOOK THE CONCEPT OF THE RANDOM SQUARE BACK TO THEIR WORKPLACE** and made it a part of their everyday decision making. They would bring in a smaller version of the physical card square and lay it in the center of the table during their meetings. When the conversation got bogged down, someone would point to or grab and hold the blank random card, using it like a permission slip to allow more freedom in the ideas that were being surfaced. As a result, the team felt more empowered to make decisions, trusting their own creativity and problem-solving skills.

IF YOU WANT TO GET THE MOST OUT OF YOUR IMAGINATION, LET IT HAVE THE FREEDOM TO ROAM WITH SOME GUIDANCE FROM YOU.

Often when we run into a roadblock, we default to our old stories from the past and let our imagination pull out the old pictures, when we were unsuccessful with a similar challenge. While we may enjoy the temporary trip down memory lane, the key to better ideas is to stop the patterned thinking and remind yourself to be curious. Remind yourself to approach this with the same enthusiasm you had when you were learning a new skill as a child before the story of "**YOU'RE NOT CREATIVE ENOUGH**" was born.

YOU MUST INVITE PRESENT-YOU TO LET GO OF PAST-YOU, SO YOU CAN INVITE IN FUTURE-YOU WHO SEES A MORE POSITIVE OUTCOME TO THE CURRENT SITUATION YOU ARE IN. Doing so, you clear a path of your inner Creative Genius solution-focused voice to come through.

LET'S PUT IT TO TEST.

If you want to see how your imagination works, right now, replay a situation that you wish you had handled a little better. Something simple, like the problem you have with your dog who always pulls on his leash. (Confession — that's my problem.) What's your standard response?

If you're like me, you may yank on the leash, doing your best to physically pull your dog. For those of you who are not dog owners, this is known as the **YANK AND CRANK METHOD** of dog training: it has been proven time and time again to be **HIGHLY INEFFECTIVE**. The harder you pull in one direction, the harder your dog pulls in another, resulting in an incessant pattern of tug of war.

Let's take this method for dog walking and see if we can find a better outcome. If your negative bias has its way, you will replay this power play with your dog over and over. Sometimes you'll win, sometimes your dog will. Either way, it's exhausting.

Because your brain is wired to use negative bias as the default mode of responding, when you try to make a change, it sees no options but the one in front of you. You tell yourself to pull harder and maybe this time your dog will respond differently.

THE PATTERN DOESN'T CHANGE BECAUSE THERE IS NO RANDOM SQUARE IN THE GAME TO GENERATE THE POSSIBILITY FOR SOMETHING DIFFERENT TO HAPPEN!

If you really want things to be different, you must change the way you approach the entire situation by imagining a scenario with a better outcome. Imagine the moment your dog reaches the end of his leash and begins to tug. What dog trainers tell you to do in this situation is to turn on your heel and walk in a different direction so your dog, unsure of what is happening, has no choice but to follow you. That's right, you take the lead and direct the outcome. And your dog, no longer finding you a willing player in the old game, follows along.

HAVING IMAGINED A DIFFERENT SCENARIO, you are now back out on the street, your dog begins to pull and instead of following the same old script, you play out the scene in the way you imagined it in your mind with this new outcome. If you slip and feel yourself going back to your old way of doing something, try to remind yourself of the new possibilities you've created by saying something out loud, like "**SHIFT**" or "**CHANGE**."

So why do this? I am encouraging you to first imagine a situation and then give it a different outcome because neuroscientists have found that your brain doesn't know the difference between what you have imagined and what you have done. Imagination is a powerful tool for creating the solutions you desire.

In fact, your imagination is so powerful it can trick your brain into believing you have already done something. In studies where people imagined in great detail doing some form of physical work-out on a regular basis (while not doing any exercise at all) they all increased their physical strength! Gymnasts use this technique all the time too — they visualize themselves doing those complex double-twists and layouts long before they actually give it a try. By the time they do, their body already believes it is possible.

The implications are clear; you can create positive outcomes by using your imagination to create changes in your health, financial well-being, work satisfaction and relationships. It may even save you some money on a gym membership!

To make the most of your brain's way of learning new techniques, it may be helpful to understand how our brains work.

When I first began using visual imaging in my work with corporate groups I would be at a loss when people used concepts like **"CONNECTION"** or **"ORGANIC GROWTH"** to describe their processes. Because I was working in real time, drawing images as the group talked, I struggled to create an image for abstract terms and usually ended up simply writing the word. **UNDER PRESSURE, MY MIND WOULD GO BLANK,** and I couldn't conjure up any images.

During breaks I'd quickly scan for images on my phone to get ideas for pictures I could draw. Over time, I became more confident and simply relaxed, leaving a space on the drawing and searching the web, then circling back to drop in that image later. As a result, I found that within a few months of retraining myself to consistently relax, search and deposit, new images just came to me and with little hesitation, I was able to quickly draw them.

As I expanded the number of images I had to choose from, I found I was able to rewire my brain so that it paid more attention to images in general, that way it could effortlessly supply me with a steady stream of them whenever necessary.

Then I realized that if I wasn't careful, I repeatedly drew the same images over and over. I had to feed my brain with new images by looking at a variety of drawings by other artists. Only then was I able to quickly access newer images that matched the abstract concepts being used.

In some ways what I was doing was engaging three distinct parts of my brain.

1. By looking at lots of images I was providing my hippocampus (the memory center of my brain that stores images) many possibilities to be used when I needed to depict abstract concepts. The hippocampus received this constant flow of images, storing some, based on added sensory stimulus like touch, taste, smell, sight, sound, and others it simply discarded. When I looked through a book of images or online cartoon images and **THEN ATTACHED IT TO A WORD IN MY MIND** or even added a feeling or story to it, I had a wider catalogue of ideas for my pre-frontal cortex to play with later.

2. The **PRE-FRONTAL CORTEX** helps with combining images together for problem solving or brainstorming during a specific moment in time. The interaction between it and the hippocampus is like a railroad: the **HIPPOCAMPUS** lays down new tracks — creating and grabbing old memories — while the prefrontal cortex switches between the

tracks, grabbing related memories to create context for an experience. The resulting memory is brief unless you attach feeling or importance to it.

3. Then, all I had to do was keep my amygdala in check. Sometimes I wasn't sure if what I drew looked like what it needed to and then my worrying got amped up by my amygdala which is in a constant battle to protect me. "**DOES THAT PICTURE I DREW LOOK ANYTHING LIKE A CROWN? I HOPE SO! STAY CALM, STAY CALM.**" Your amygdala activates when you are scared, since it's linked to the "flight or fight response," but it works directly with the pre-frontal cortex which helps provide reasoning for why the situation might not be such a big deal. That's why **TAKING A DEEP BREATH WHEN YOU ARE NERVOUS HELPS**. It gives your nervous system a break, and you the chance to nudge yourself towards more positive thoughts.

By knowing how these three parts of the brain work, I found I could strengthen their ability to work together by providing what they each needed. That could be reassurance or focused attention or a new bank of images to pull from. Subsequently I was able to keep my mind open to the steady stream of imagery, drawing whatever came to me, and turning down the volume on my worry or internal critic.

I'm now so comfortable with this I can easily make light of the situation if I can't think of an image, or the image looks weird. Interestingly enough, this maps to what happens in your brain as you get better with any skill. At first you use your prefrontal cortex to come up with the solution — which is all around problem solving to get you out of trouble, later you tap into the temporal lobe which allows you greater access to abstract information.

When you understand how your brain works, **YOU CAN BEGIN TO DO SPECIFIC THINGS TO ENHANCE BOTH ITS ABILITY TO ADAPT TO NEW EXPERIENCES AND ABSORB INFORMATION**. Neuroscientist David Eagleman suggests that your brain allows itself to be shaped by the details of your life experience. He uses the term "live-wired" to describe this phenomenon. While genes provide general directions for neural networks, your life experience provides the fine-tuning that allows your brain to adapt to specific elements unique to you. This "live wiring" process continues throughout your life. Your brain never stops adapting and changing so it only makes sense to do everything you can to keep it flexible, and to use it to your full advantage.

PROGRAMMING YOUR BRAIN

Imagination helps you resolve and initiate what cognitive neuroscientist Alex Schlegel calls "**MENTAL WORKSPACE**." This he describes as a widespread neural network that coordinates activity across several regions in the brain and consciously manipulates symbols, images, ideas and theories.

He proposes that if you can reliably access this mental workspace to solve and resolve problems, you shift your perception of who you are in the present moment, as well as the person you hope to be in the future. **THE FUTURE-YOU CONCEPT** is so compelling that if students knew that imagining the most fantastic future-self possible would help them make better decisions in the here and now, they would become inspired to try new things and take bigger risks in their choices. I am not referring to driving fast or taking risks that might endanger your life here. I'm referring to risk-taking to challenge your thinking or to increase your capacity to do or be better in a sport, or learning a language or a skill, or speaking up in a meeting.

For example, imagine that you want something, like a shift in your career to do that thing you have always dreamed about. You need to figure out how to get up the courage to step out of your current life to do it.

The wise thing to do would be to create a savings plan rather than just quitting your job, hoping that somehow, miraculously, you'd find enough money to support your family and pay your mortgage. But **YOU CAN CREATE THE SEEMINGLY IMPOSSIBLE BY START-ING WITH IMAGINING A FUTURE-YOU**, who is acting on that stage or building the next high-tech solution. The excitement and chemistry that dreaming of that future-you creates in your body will help you come up with new ideas that you want to capture so you can act upon them.

To engage the parts of your brain that are responsible for live wiring new ways of approaching a challenge, you might start by getting a bunch of brightly colored Post-It® notes and writing on each, one idea for how to create the shift into the new you.

Your ideas might include reaching out across your network to meet new people or putting a percentage of weekly earnings in a savings account to build up a pool of cash if an in-between period of income occurs. But something different might also drop in, like selling that old car for instance, to use it for seed money for your idea.

The goal is to brainstorm lots of ideas. Your imagination thrives on visual data, whether that's images you draw, or just a bunch of scribbled ideas on colored paper. **SEEING EVERYTHING SPREAD OUT BEFORE YOU INVITES YOUR CREATIVE GENIUS TO GET INVOLVED** and start seeing new ways to make your plans a reality.

DON'T WORRY ABOUT HAVING A CONCRETE PLAN TO START WITH. THE POINT OF THIS EXERCISE IS TO LET YOUR IMAGINATION TAKE THE LEAD IN CREATING IDEAS.

When people create images — by drawing simple pictures — of their current state and possible outcomes, they are often surprised when something in the picture emerges that they didn't expect, or a pattern for action suddenly becomes very clear.

Doing this kind of exercise is based on the "**YES… AND**" principle, a technique for improving the brainstorming and creativity process.

While our typical response is to focus on all the obstacles in the way of reaching a goal, our inner censor will be sending messages like, "**YOU DON'T KNOW THE FIRST THING ABOUT CYBERSECURITY, WHAT MAKES YOU THINK YOU COULD LEARN THAT?**" or "**IF I BRING THIS UP WITH MY PARTNER, SHE'S GOING TO FLIP OUT!**"

The "**YES… AND**" principle works on the belief that first you must say an emphatic "**YES!**" to any idea that you dream up. Then you let your brain engage in flexible decision making, until you can clearly see the options that could bring you closer to that future-you.

IT IS IMPORTANT THAT YOU DON'T CENSOR YOURSELF or allow a negative voice to shoot down anything that might help you problem solve, brainstorm ideas, or sell yourself or your services. Don't worry about how your ideas fit into the bigger picture. That process takes place in another part of the brain responsible for rational thinking. Save that for after you have come up with all your ideas.

You can't access a free flow of creativity at the same time as you're critiquing and editing. This is why lots of successful, brilliant writers still do their writing the old school way, with pen and paper, rather than a computer, where the flow may be impeded.

The critical thinking function of your brain wants to filter everything through grammar and spell check, while the hand/brain connection generates pure flow of creativity.

THE LANGUAGE OF YOUR CREATIVE GENIUS
IS A RICH STREAM OF FRUITFUL IDEAS
THAT MAY BE A CRAZY COMBINATION
OF BRILLIANT, SILLY AND THOUGHT PROVOKING.

When this tap is flowing, things move quickly, and you would be foolish to stop and critique or correct what is coming through. Your task is to let it flow until it's exhausted. **THE GOAL OF THE CREATIVE GENIUS EQUATION IS TO HELP YOU FIND WAYS TO OPEN THE TAP AND KEEP IT FLOWING.** Your brain, that ever-expansive live wiring machine, is a fertile environment with limitless potential for creativity. And there are proven methods for making this happen.

Meditation is a perfect example of a way to help yourself relax and let your imagination flourish. In fact, groups that meditated before brainstorming had a higher ratio of ideas. Your task is to keep your garden plot fertile by practicing basic self-care — getting enough sleep, drinking plenty of water, balancing work with play, daydreaming, as well as actively engaging your imagination.

IMAGINATION AFFECTS OUTCOME

Our perception of ourselves and the world around us is profoundly affected by imagination. We often think about the things we imagine and the things we perceive as being distinct and separate. However, studies show that our imagination of a sound or a shape changes how we perceive the world around us just as it would if we heard or saw it in actuality. Christopher Berger discovered that "...**WHAT WE IMAGINE HEARING CAN CHANGE WHAT WE ACTUALLY SEE, AND WHAT WE IMAGINE SEEING CAN CHANGE WHAT WE ACTUALLY HEAR.**"

My experience shows that what we imagine ourselves experiencing or becoming works in the same way. By actively working with your imagination, you open yourself to new ideas, solutions and what you want or need to create to move yourself forward into a better you in the future.

TRY THIS FOR YOURSELF

Imagine it's one week from today. On that day, what do you want to have accomplished or created? Start to **COME UP WITH THREE PROJECTS THAT YOU WANT TO HAVE COMPLETED BY THE END OF THE DAY, ONE WEEK FROM NOW.** The projects can be mundane or awe-inspiring. This is a perfect technique to try with something you have been putting off.

Once you have clear idea of what you want, draw a picture of it. This should be a sketch (**NOTHING FANCY**) but be sure it is an image that clearly conveys to you what your goal is.

TAKE A MOMENT TO IMAGINE WHAT YOU WILL FEEL LIKE HAVING COMPLETED THAT GOAL, WHAT THE FINISHED PRODUCT WILL LOOK LIKE AND HOW YOU AND THOSE AROUND YOU WILL RESPOND TO THE PROJECT HAVING BEEN COMPLETED.

To activate your goal, go forward as if what you have imagined and drawn is on its way. Assume a positive outcome and let the magic of the universe close the gap. Don't forget though, to tie up your wagon with action. Schedule time in your calendar to fulfill that vision in a way that works best for you. For me, for example, if I put pressure on myself by moving the deadline to a date as close as I can, I am able to heighten my ability to get it done. That may not work for you — you might prefer a more measured approach. Either way, plan for the project to be completed.

DERAILING AND REROUTING FEAR

Part of your imaginative process is linked to your fear response and negative bias. Whatever fears you have, they will generate images that remind you of the possibility of failure, either based on your own past experiences or borrowed from stories you may have seen or heard from others. Like a broken record, the synapses in your brain play these bad scenes repeatedly, drawing from a memory that has been hardwired into your brain's neural network.

Neurologist Robert Barton found that our brains reward us with dopamine, a neurotransmitter that is activated when something happens unexpectedly, whenever we recognize and complete patterns.

Stories are one example of patterns. The brain recognizes the familiar structure of a story, with a beginning, middle and end, and it rewards us for clearing up the ambiguity. Here's the bad news… **THIS REWARD SYSTEM WORKS JUST AS WELL WHEN WE IMAGINE A NEGATIVE ENDING**.

You must interrupt that negative bias before it tosses you down the slippery slope. **BRENE' BROWN SUGGESTS THAT JUST STOPPING TO BE PRESENT CAN SHIFT THE EMOTION**. Then you can further uncouple yourself from the fearful or negative story simply by getting curious about it. Where did the story come from? Where do you feel it in your body? **YOUR IMAGINATION IS UNDER YOUR CONTROL**. You can direct its focus like a spotlight, on what you want to highlight or explore.

THE MORE LIGHT YOU SHINE, THE CLEARER THE IMAGE BECOMES.

Your imagination, left to its own devices, tends to drift around, randomly focusing on this or that, so it needs direction. When you use it as a tool to explore what you want to know more about, it will give you better options for which step to take on the path towards the things you desire. You can harness it to trick yourself into taking bigger risks and when you have any measure of success, you will rewire your brain with courage and leave the old you behind.

When people draw their future, they create small images of the most amazing things that they want to see happen.

AN ESSENTIAL PART OF THE PROCESS IS TO "DOUBLE CLICK" ON OBJECTS AND EXPERIENCES FOR YOUR DESIRED NEW REALITY AND USE YOUR IMAGINATION TO FEEL THEM FULLY AS IF THEY ARE HAPPENING RIGHT NOW.

Heightened feeling and images are the glue that you use to solidify that memory into your hippocampus and program your neurons in a new way. Remember, the brain doesn't know the difference between what you did and what you imagined, so it is already living this new future you, now.

When you start using these techniques to access **CREATIVE GENIUS YOU** for changes both big and small, it's not uncommon to feel that it must not be working when things don't seem to be changing very quickly. While I am firmly convinced that anyone who works with their imagination to access their creativity and generate solutions to their problems can expect changes, the pace at which they occur can sometimes feel frustrating.

There might be a multitude of reasons, but often it is as simple as not having created enough focus and momentum by celebrating the small shifts you are making. You might also be holding on to some limiting beliefs about who you are or what you are capable of. In fact if your vision involves other people, those people have to come into alignment with the vision as well.

It is helpful to remember that everything has its own timing and check if you are focusing too much or too little on outcomes. We each have unique obstacles to navigate for every goal we want to achieve.

I believe that what often happens when we don't immediately get what we want is that we start to second-guess ourselves and, as a result, **MISS THE SUBTLE OPPORTUNITIES** that are presenting themselves in every moment.

I have learned something from the feedback I've received from people who watched my **DRAW YOUR FUTURE®, TEDX** video. Those who have had the most success imagining the changes they wanted to create by using images of their journey had one other thing in common: they kept on going, activating the **DRIVE** part of the **CREATIVE GENIUS EQUATION**. Often, they would revisit their goals again and again, playing it out in their minds eye, until they saw the obstacles or opportunities in a new way. In time, their limited thinking fell away and made room for the free flow of solutions always available through the imaginative faculties. I'll explain why when we get to Desire.

Your imagination is one of the most powerful tools at your disposal and it's on 24/7. When you consciously use it in a focused and clear way, the possibilities for new ways to achieve change are infinite.

QUICK RECAP BEFORE WE MOVE ON

1. Asking questions stimulates your imagination. **CURIOSITY WILL OPEN A STEADY STREAM OF NEW POSSIBILITIES.**

Be sure to capture them on Post-its® or draw them, so your brain can just be an open tap and not have to worry about remembering them all.

2. **YOU CAN REPROGRAM YOUR BRAIN** to overcome your negative bias and use this mental workspace to focus on and create a future you.

3. Use your imagination to **ACTIVELY IMPACT THE OUTCOME** of an experience by imagining it first. Imagination can change what you see or hear in advance of the experience.

4. **REROUTE YOUR FEAR** by daydreaming the best-case scenario in your mind. Your imagination is under your control. You can direct its focus like a spotlight, on what you want to highlight or explore. You may be surprised at what new things you'll uncover.

EXERCISE: IMAGINATION — YOUR POWER AND PREDICTOR

In your journal, identify a challenge or a bold step you are facing or taking right now. Describe it and express how you feel about it. Then, having expressed it, take a few deep breaths and then answer the following questions:

- **WHAT IS THIS CHALLENGE TEACHING ME?**

- **HOW IS THIS FAMILIAR TO SOMETHING I'VE EXPERIENCED OR SEEN BEFORE?**

Now, let your mind go and list at least 20 possible solutions to solve it. It doesn't matter how wild they might seem at first. Ignore any messages from your brain saying, "**YOU CAN'T DO THAT!**" while you list them.

MARVEL IN YOUR ABILITY TO CREATE SOLUTIONS TO ANY PROBLEM. AND, OF COURSE, IF ONE OR MORE OF THOSE SOLUTIONS IS VIABLE RIGHT NOW, GO DO IT!

Now choose the top 3 most provocative ideas and rank their plausibility on a scale from 0 (not plausible) to 5 (very plausible):

1.

2.

3.

Add in a random element by asking: **WHAT COULD POSSIBLY HELP ME HAVE A BREAKTHROUGH IN ACTIVATING MY TOP CHOICE?**

Bring in an invisible (and helpful) friend by imagining you are sitting across from a historic figure who could help you resolve this and ask their advice. Write down their answer.

3. INTUITION

Intuition is the ability to sense and know something that you can't explain with facts. It's a subtle voice, a nudge inside you, that is guided by a strong feeling. It's most obvious when you are about to do something you might regret: when you share some gossip, for example, and you feel a tiny brake on your words, so suddenly you stop talking and close your mouth, or when you're driving home and decide to take a different route only to find that you've just missed getting caught it a big traffic jam.

MOST PEOPLE FIND THAT, THE MORE THEY LEARN TO TRUST AND FOLLOW THEIR INTUITIVE SENSE, THE MORE SEEMINGLY MAGICAL SYNCHRONICITY THEY EXPERIENCE IN THEIR EVERYDAY LIFE.

Things happen as if out of the blue and usually create a positive after-glow that enhances a feeling of connectivity to something bigger.

Intuition is a sensory experience that happens instinctively. For some people it's something they feel, for others it's something they hear. When people describe how their intuition somehow guided them, they often say, "I JUST KNEW," or they have a "GUT FEELING."

While some people regard intuition as unreliable, it's grounded in information gleaned from past experiences — a mash up of knowledge and wisdom. It's your brain on autopilot, tuning into information outside of your conscious awareness. It taps into the river of the energy fields around and within you and, like your imagi-nation, intuition can be focused and fine-tuned for greater reliability.

Neurobiological research has discovered a complex communication system between the millions of neurons embedded in the stomach walls and the limbic brain that is key to our decision-making.

In studies about food choices, when people were asked to use their intuition when choosing what to eat, they made better decisions about which food would be healthier for them.

THE LIMBIC SYSTEM
IS RESPONSIBLE FOR
THE EXPERIENCE AND EXPRESSION
OF EMOTION.
IT IS WHERE
OUR HABITS AND
BEHAVIORAL PATTERNS
ARE STORED,
SO THE GUT-BRAIN
HELPS GOVERN
NOT ONLY THE HEALTHY FUNCTIONING
OF OUR DIGESTIVE SYSTEM
BUT ALSO
COMPLEX BRAIN FUNCTIONS INCLUDING
MOTIVATION AND ACCESS
TO OUR DEEPER WISDOM.

TARA SWART
SECRETS OF THE UNIVERSE,
THE SCIENCE OF THE BRAIN

BEFORE YOU DISMISS THE FEELING IN YOUR GUT THAT ALERTS YOUR SENSES, KNOW THAT IT IS ONE OF THE MOST POWERFUL AND DISCERNING TOOLS YOU POSSESS.

Intuition is a key part of your Creative Genius superpower. It relies on billions of bits of information stored in our brain and body to generate guidance and sometimes warnings.

A story I often tell is about a friend who was living in Thailand in 2004. One morning as he headed out to walk his dog, he suddenly got a strong feeling that he should take the trail up the mountain instead of down to his usual beach walk. A short time later, a powerful tsunami hit the west side of Thailand covering the beaches with a monumental wall of water that swallowed everything. Had he not followed his intuition that urged him to do things differently, he and his dog would have been dragged into the ocean.

Though you may struggle to understand exactly how your intuition works, it's hard to deny the huge role it plays in your everyday life. Intuition is a quiet inner voice that constantly sends you messages and always operates in your best interest. Steve Jobs famously called intuition **"MORE POWERFUL THAN INTELLECT."** Albert Einstein credited intuition with being our most valuable asset and one of our most unused senses. He described it as a **"FEELING FOR THE ORDER LYING BEHIND THE APPEARANCE OF SOMETHING."**

Call it what you will — gut feeling, sixth sense, innate wisdom, inner voice — it's an integral factor in developing **CREATIVE GENIUS YOU,** helping you sort and sift through options when making decisions or developing new ideas.

In her book, **THRIVE,** *Huffington Post* founder Arianna Huffington reminds us that our intuition is always there, always reading the situation, always trying to steer us the right way. But do we hear it? Are we paying attention? Feeding and nurturing our intuition is no doubt key way to our ability to thrive, at work and in life.

If it's so integral, how can you develop it further? Studies have found that intuition is enhanced when you are in an "alpha" or relaxed state of inquiry, as opposed to the "beta" state of mind where most of us

live in our day to day, managing worries or participating in Zoom calls at a frenzied pace. Our brain generally operates in either a state of abstraction (calm, go-with-the-flow or daydreaming) or we are in a state of control, using our analytical mind to problem solve, work with worry, or focus on goal getting. Abstraction is a gateway to intuition, so getting quiet is key to enhancing and strengthening your capacity to hear and trust your intuition.

WHEN YOU ARE UP AGAINST A CHALLENGE OR NEED TO MAKE A CHOICE, SIMPLY STOPPING TO TUNE IN TO YOUR BODY WILL HELP YOU BECOME MORE RECEPTIVE TO SOLUTIONS SURFACING.

Another aspect of accessing your intuition has to do with that gut-brain connection and the chemistry in your gut. Healthy biomes play a key role in your ability to sense your intuition. Just as having a cold or experiencing pain inhibits your ability to think clearly, the well-being of your digestive system allows you to think better.

In a study in the Netherlands, probiotic supplementation was shown to alter and enhance mood. Who knew that taking probiotics would help you think and tune in to your sixth sense better!

TURN UP THE VOLUME ON YOUR INTUITION

Getting quiet enough to listen is the first step, but here are three additional suggestions for ways to turn up the volume on your intuition:

1. Open up lines of communication with your intuition by **ASKING FOR A CLEAR SIGN.** You can write down your ask on a piece of paper or simply ask it inside yourself. If you are alone, you might voice your ask out loud. You can also

carry it in your pocket to remember what you have asked your intuition to help you with.

2. **KEEP A JOURNAL** with you to help you pay attention to any guidance or nudges you feel. They might be physical sensations or some other very tangible feeling. There might be a road sign you pass or words in a song that you are listening to. It might be as simple as someone saying something random to you at the grocery store but their words, for some reason, stand out and relate to your question or request. It's like someone took a highlighter to a moment or feeling in your day. Write these things down. It will alert your brain that these subtle messages are important.

3. **ACT ON WHAT YOUR INTUITION IS GUIDING YOU TO DO** and see what happens. Ask to be guided on how to handle a situation in your everyday life. Start with something simple like, "**WHERE SHOULD WE GO FOR DINNER TONIGHT?**" Then listen for a subtle tug in one direction or another. Intuitive knowing starts with raising your awareness to what is already occurring. Ask first, then test out what you are

being guided to do. Sometimes you might get an urge to call someone on the phone or send someone an email. If they respond with, "**I WAS JUST THINKING ABOUT YOU**," **KAPOW!** Maybe they really needed to talk to someone, and you were that person showing up out of the blue. Training yourself to follow through on subtle, intuitive clues will not only heighten your awareness of what is happening in the moment, it will also build your confidence in yourself and your choices. Intuition is the bridge to the subtle seemingly "**COINCIDENTAL**" things that happen. Review your journal regularly to notice any patterns between the times you relied on your intuition and the outcomes. You may be surprised by what you'll see and how often you are missing out on key messaging.

Developing your intuition is a powerful way to build your self-confidence. It shows you that you're capable of knowing what's right for you. When you act on the guidance from your intuition, you increase the insights and decrease your anxiety and self-doubt: two big obstacles to creativity and effective problem solving.

WHEN YOU ARE STRESSED, YOUR BRAIN IS OPERATING FROM ITS LIZARD-LIKE FIGHT-OR-FLIGHT STATE, EVEN IF IT'S ONLY A LITTLE STRESSED.

When you stop, take a few deep breaths, calm it down and you'll be able to listen better and open the drapes on the stage of your pre-frontal cortex, your brain's problem solver.

Intuition is your own unique and powerful way to activate **CREATIVE GENIUS YOU**. It's that ever-present sixth sense just waiting to guide you. When you invite your intuition to help you make decisions, especially when you are contemplating big life changes, you make room for doors to open that hold more potential than you currently know about. Those tips will give you a place to funnel your passion and focus your drive.

INTUITION APPLIED TO GOAL GETTING

Your Creative Genius relies on inner nudges to help guide you to the best possible outcome for every decision you make.

Daniel Kahneman, Ph.D. received the Nobel Prize in Economics for his research on the use of intuition versus rational thought and its impact on economic decision-making. He found that unconscious thought processes powerfully determine many aspects of our life, from how we perceive and react to other people, to how we make decisions.

When we allow our imagination to mockup possible ways to problem solve, we can then pivot all those possibilities to our intuition and actively use it to help us choose the best course of action. In my previous book, **DRAWING SOLUTIONS**, I walked through my mapping process to help individuals, teams and businesses make change more easily. Those that found the most success were people who called on their intuition to help them create what I refer to as the "**3 BOLD STEPS**."

These steps will help you get off your butt to bridge the gap between where you are and where to want to be. The highest success rate came from those who used at least one of the following signs to determine what the biggest and boldest steps should be:

- **A GUT FEELING** or emotional response

- **AN INNER VOICE** that suggested a course of action

- **A PHYSICAL SENSATION** (a tug at their heart or tightening in their 3rd eye between the eyebrows)

- **AN INSTANT KNOWING** of what to do: "**I JUST KNEW THIS WAS THE RIGHT STEP.**"

Intuition gives you a sense of what you feel will work, might be fun, could possibly help expand you or your team, lead you to a new career or to a new relationship. Intuition serves up the opportunities that align with your authentic self. **BUT YOU MUST BE CURIOUS.**

Curiosity magnifies the senses about the information you are getting and then helps you explore with openness what you are discovering. At first, what you find might not always be the exact solution, but it often points you toward your next step. With practical and deliberate application, you will notice a sometimes-dramatic difference in your ability to consciously understand the unconscious workings in yourself and your world.

Recognizing the flow of intuition in daily life takes practice. Most of the time you and I believe that **WHAT WE THINK** is more important than what our intuition is telling us and subsequently try to think our way through life's decisions. Thought is limited and driven by ego, yet it is compulsive. It will often steer you down a path that reinforces your fear, giving power to it and limiting what you believe is possible.

Consider this: every day you have millions of thoughts, most of them subconscious. And most of us never give them the attention they deserve. We either dismiss important ideas and let them pass by or we fail to notice and stop those that take us down the slippery slope to past beliefs and stories about ourselves and others that no longer apply to who we are and life we are living.

In an interview, Kristina Kuzmic shared that there is nothing wrong with having insecurities, it is just that we give them far too much authority. In contrast, intuition is rooted in our deepest self, what some refer to as the timeless essence of our being.

SO HOW DO YOU KNOW, WHEN YOU ASK FOR GUIDANCE ON SOMETHING, IF THE RESPONSE IS BEING DRIVEN BY YOUR INTUITION OR YOUR EGO?

THE DIFFERENCE IS SIMPLY IN HOW IT MAKES YOU FEEL. If the resulting nudge comes from a place of fear: fear of not being loved or seen or heard or valued, no matter the result, it's probably your ego. If it doesn't scare you, it's usually coming from a place of love.

WHEN YOUR EGO IS SPEAKING TO YOU, THE ENERGY FEELS TENSE AND CONTRACTED. WITH INTUITION, THE ENERGY IS EXPANSIVE AND UPLIFTING.

This is true of your incessant subconscious thoughts running amok. Thoughts running amok are the ones that generally make you feel insecure or bad about yourself. Your intuition is a tip giver, there to help enhance your life, guide you and provide insight and help when you need it. Ego, on the other hand, is a tip taker, pulling you down the slippery slope into thinking all of your ideas are worthless and will lead you nowhere.

To build your intuitive muscle further, you want to develop your ability to act on your nudges immediately and circumvent the mind's interpretation. In Anne Archer Butcher's book **INNER GUIDANCE: OUR DIVINE BIRTH RIGHT**, she cites numerous experiences where direct guidance saved her life, noting, "**INNER GUIDANCE IS FAST, INSTINCTUAL DIALOGUE FROM THE SOURCE OF LIFE THAT OFFERS A SOLUTION.**" Once, as a teacher, she was about to write a quote from Thoreau, when her intuition guided her to write a series of sentences on the board for her students to discuss.

> "MY OPINION IS THAT IN THE WORLD OF KNOWLEDGE THE IDEA OF GOOD APPEARS LAST OF ALL, AND IS SEEN ONLY WITH AN EFFORT; AND, WHEN SEEN IS ALSO INFERRED TO BE THE UNIVERSAL AUTHOR OF ALL THINGS BEAUTIFUL AND RIGHT, PARENT OF LIGHT OF THE LORD OF LIGHT IN THIS VISIBLE WORLD."

SHE HAD NO IDEA WHERE THE QUOTE HAD COME FROM, IT LITERALLY CAME THROUGH HER HAND. She said the directive didn't feel like a choice; it was as though a force moved through her and she followed. Because she followed her own curiosity, both she and her students shared a powerful learning experience that she said probably would not have been possible had she thought about it. The egocentric part of herself would have chosen a safer exercise.

Later, the librarian helped her identify the quote as one from Plato, in a book she had never even heard of. But the conversations with her class stemming from that nudge were incredible, taking them into a deep discussion.

When you choose to listen to your intuition and learn to leave the ego and its self-interest behind, you clear the path for your better self to step forward. Intuition links you to open to a deeper understanding and experience with the broader mystery behind the eternal questions: Why am I here? What is my life purpose? What can I do in this moment to keep in alignment with who I am as a person and the unique gifts I bring to the world?

As a result, you become more aligned with what some people refer to as your "true North" and you step into a powerful interactive adventure with yourself and your life. You find yourself taking on the role of the explorer, looking for clues leading you towards a deeper experience of life, work, relationships, and interests you desire.

WHEN YOU INVITE YOUR INTUITION INTO THE PROCESS, YOU WILL SENSE THE SUBTLE DIFFERENCE BETWEEN WHAT YOUR EGO THINKS IS "BEST" FOR YOU AND TRUE INNER GUIDANCE.

Your ego is tricky and sly — always wanting you to come out "on top," but with practice you can come to feel how much more expansive and inclusive your decisions are when they're based on intuition.

When you look at the world around us, a lot of the decisions are really coming from this self-centered "it's all about me (versus we)" space.

What you imagine and what you choose to act on are very different based on who's driving the bus. Your imagination's job is to serve up all the options without judgment.

Here's an example: You are thinking about how to educate your child during a temporary school closure and, if you have the money, you are thinking, "**LET'S HIRE A TEACHER FOR THE HOME PART OF THE SCHOOL WEEK. MAYBE I'LL INVITE THE NEIGHBORS' KIDS TOO**." You are not thinking about people outside your comfort zone, who might benefit from that kind of a circumstance, but can't afford it. You might get a nudge to invite disadvantaged students along too but your ego overrides it. ("**WHAT WOULD THE NEIGHBORS THINK?**")

Our intuition's role is to help guide our decision making for the highest good and sometimes we forget that. When you become aware of who's driving your decisions, then you invite your imagination and intuition to become the dynamic duo they were meant to be. Once they team up, you start to imagine bigger and better and you free your imagination to travel into the unknown areas, where you will take bigger risks and subsequently reap bigger rewards.

HAND IN HAND, BY TAKING YOUR FEAR AND YOUR EGO OUT OF THE EQUATION, YOU OPEN THE DOOR FOR YOUR IMAGINATION AND INTUITION TO SET YOU UP FOR SUCCESS IN ALIGNMENT WITH YOUR TRUE PURPOSE.

Leveraging this part of the **CREATIVE GENIUS EQUATION: IMAGINATION X INTUITION,** you discover critical information that often leads to new choices and options. Watch for the possibilities that fill you with excitement (**DESIRE**), then you'll naturally find the drive (**SWEAT**) needed to complete the task.

QUICK RECAP BEFORE WE MOVE ON

1. Intuition is a sensory experience that happens instinctively.

2. Gut and brain linkage is an essential component for your ability to sense and make better decisions.

3. You can turn up the volume on your intuition just by being aware of who is driving the bus.

4. When you set your intuition free it unlocks your imagination to be even more creative.

EXERCISE: LISTENING TO AND APPLYING YOUR INTUITION

You need to be ready to listen to your intuition and that takes a bit of practice. Start to keep a journal or a stack of Post-it® notes handy and notice every time you "feel" an intuitive nudge. Tune in to these nudges and observe:

1. What choice were you making?

2. How important was the choice?

3. How confident were you about listening to your intuition?

4. What is one thing you could do right now to up your intuition?

ONE OF THE MOST
POWERFUL WELLSPRINGS
OF CREATIVE ENERGY,
OUTSTANDING ACCOMPLISHMENT
AND SELF-FULFILLMENT
SEEMS TO BE
FALLING IN LOVE
WITH SOMETHING—
YOUR DREAM,
YOUR IMAGE OF THE FUTURE...

E. PAUL TORRANCE

4. DESIRE

Desire is often referred to as the feeling you get when you are strongly wishing for or wanting something. It's correlated with feelings of longing, anticipation and expectation. Some desires are easily fulfilled, like an ice-cream cone on a hot day, but others might seem too risky and may be silenced or ignored, sometimes for years. These unexpressed desires may go underground but they rarely go away. The **CREATIVE GENIUS EQUATION** can help you bring to the surface desires that you may have kept secret, perhaps for a long, long time.

Often in my mapping work, people tell me about their secret desires. It may be the career they never pursued or a talent they knew they had but were never encouraged to take seriously. We all have desires we've pushed down and neglected.

You may have deferred your dreams because of your other responsibilities, telling yourself that "SOMEDAY, WHEN THE KIDS ARE OLDER," or "WHEN I HAVE ENOUGH SAVINGS," or… then I will _____ (fill in the blank). Whatever the reason, your dream is still there waiting for you, tucked away as your secret desire.

My TEDx DRAW YOUR FUTURE® video inspired many people to make a change and surface that dormant part of themselves. One viewer, let's call her Melinda, wrote:

IN MY IMAGINATION I SAW MYSELF AS A DREAM CATCHING / IMAGINATION / VISIONARY COACH WHO COULD TEACH PEOPLE ONE BY ONE TO LIVE AN AMAZING, OVER-THE-TOP LIFE AND TO HELP THEM TO ERASE THE PRISON WALLS OF THEIR MIND ON THEIR DRAWING OF THE FUTURE. THAT

PICTURE FUELED MY DESIRE UNTIL I MADE THAT DREAM MY REALITY.

EXACTLY HOW DID SHE MAKE IT HAPPEN? She started by imagining her future self. Then she put pen to paper, drawing it out, playing out the scenario of her future in her mind. Then she began acting on that future. If she ever felt discouraged or down, she said she went back to the picture and embellished it with all the best possible outcomes, adding color and additional images. Meanwhile, she kept taking small steps, each step chipping away at any obstacle that was between her and her future self, until the day she was that person.

That's an awesome story and I have thousands just like it.

Others, however, who followed a similar process, followed a different path when they got stuck. They began to create a false story based on all the reasons their brain made up about why this would or could never happen. Their brain replaced their image of success with one that they really didn't want: one of failure.

Your brain is a pattern-making machine and, unfortunately, it only follows your attention. You easily confuse it by creating the disconnect between what you desire and who you believe you are in the current moment. When this discord happens your brain reverts to old, familiar patterns of thinking and acting based on what you have done before, using well established neural pathways. It tries to turn you away from risk and back to your safety zone.

YOU CAN BREAK FROM THE PAST to move in a new direction like Melinda, by tapping into your reservoir of desire. Desire is like rocket fuel for your motivation. A colleague told me that when she was trying to decide between one career move and another, she would ask herself, "**WHAT DO I REALLY, REALLY, REALLY WANT?**" She said that the first two answers that came to her were generally what she thought she should want, versus what she really wanted. She claimed that asking the same question repeatedly brought up desires she hadn't let herself freely feel before.

When you imagine a positive future that electrifies you and sparks your Creative Genius, you are tapping into desire. Watching that inner, full-color fantasy and playing it over and over, helps to wire the new story of that new reality into your brain. That future-you is interested in helping you find ways to get beyond what you know and claim that future self.

IF YOU ASK THAT FUTURE SELF FOR ADVICE, IT WILL USE YOUR CREATIVITY TO HELP YOU CONNECT THE DOTS ABOUT WHAT ACTIONS YOU SHOULD TAKE NEXT.

In addition, when you fantasize, your brain hits that dopamine button and you find yourself filled with the belief that you can achieve what you desire. Believing you can is the first step to claiming any of your goals.

Daydreaming is another muscle you can exercise to change who you are right now and help you achieve your goals. In a study about daydreaming, researchers at University of California, Santa Barbara found that those who daydreamed most about the future had the highest levels of attention control and were best able to maintain their daydreams. They concluded that most of the participants had a "prospective bias" meaning that their view of the future shaped who they believed they were. When given time for self-reflection, their fantasies and daydreams turned toward the future and the pursuit of their long-term goals. Daydreams appeared to be a key component in goal achievement.

Two classical musicians moved to Florida. In the months before they moved, they'd emailed various orchestras to try to find one to play with. Once in Florida, they heard about a college orchestra in Tampa that accepted musicians from the community, so they both fired off an email. Seconds later they got a reply from the conductor. Could they be at an audition in an hour?

Grabbing their French horn and oboe, they jumped in the car and headed out, hoping they could navigate the wilds of Tampa traffic and arrive in time. As they drove along, Stan, sitting in the passenger seat, started drawing their desired goal on some scraps  of paper. He drew stick figures of them playing the oboe and the French horn in Florida, with happy faces and reeds working well! As they drove, they verbally day-dreamed about the possibilities of their new life playing in the college orchestra. When they arrived, the conductor introduced herself and apologized that she no longer had time for an audition. Instead, she invited them to sit in with the orchestra and just play along. Being skilled musicians, they jumped right in. At the end of the evening, she told them that they balanced the overall sound and blended in so well there was no need for an audition and she invited them to join the orchestra.

The pictures they drew — both actually and verbally — as they drove along, helped them stay focused on their desire to find an orchestra. It also filled them with the belief that it was possible. When desire ignites a spark and you follow your intuitive nudge with excitement and action, you light up what is possible. The more feeling you add, the better you tap into your Reticular Activating System (RAS), which starts to search out real life examples for your new future self.

The classic example of RAS is what is known as the "blue car effect." Imagine you are out with friends and Julie says, "**HEY, DO YOU NOTICE HOW YOU NEVER SEE BLUE CARS THESE DAYS?**" You all nod and agree, blue cars seem to have gone out of fashion. Next day, as you are on the way to the office it seems that all you see is blue cars. They are everywhere! So, does that mean Julie was making it up? Or some "god of blue cars" just got busy? No, that's your RAS at work. It just started ringing your mental bell every time a blue car went by, whereas before it just ignored them as unimportant.

Here's one of my favorite examples of how this process works. One of my blog readers began her experiment by simply writing the words, **"SURPRISE ME!"** along with a funny little drawing of herself with a surprised expression. In the days that followed, she began receiving offers to work on projects that were, well, surprising and beyond anything she had ever imagined. She wrote to me,

"I USED THIS PROCESS WHEN I FOUND MYSELF IN A PLACE OF FINANCIAL DISTRESS. THAT WAS A SURPRISE, ON ITS OWN, BUT IT LED ME TO A GREATER UNDERSTANDING OF THE IDEA OF BUILDING SAVINGS. I THEN APPLIED THAT METAPHOR TO OTHER PARTS OF MY LIFE SUCH AS BUILDING AND SAVING MY ENERGY, RESOURCES AND RELATIONSHIPS:

"I STARTED WITH WHAT SEEMED LIKE A VERY SIMPLE REQUEST THAT ULTIMATELY GENERATED INSIGHT THAT WAS A DEEPER, MORE LASTING EXPERIENCE THAT TRULY SURPRISED ME. AND IN THE PROCESS, I WAS ABLE TO ATTRACT WORK PROJECTS THAT I COULD NEVER HAVE EVEN THOUGHT WERE POSSIBLE."

Your RAS helps you identify and observe people who are living your desired experience right now, letting you see your desired future self in real life. Then as you add more details to your fantasy of your future self, including perhaps what you'll wear or who you'll meet, the excitement or thrill of the win will build, helping to create more focus and clarity for your dream.

It is consistent focus on a positive future you desire that rewrites your playbook, just like it did for those musicians who imagined their successful audition for that orchestra. Your focus, feeling and persistent imagining re-patterns your brain for success.

DESIRE + BELIEF

How do you maintain that spark of desire when things don't happen at the pace you think they should, and doubt starts to creep in? Doubt is often your brain's last-ditch effort to keep you from doing things differently. The story I tell about Mike Pohorly in my TEDxBend **CREATIVE GENIUS YOU** is a beautiful example of how this works.

Mike was an assistant director on many films, but his secret dream was to make a film of his own. One year, when he was shooting a commercial in Bali, he got an exciting idea for his own short film. Coincidentally, a friend had just sent him a link to **DRAW YOUR FUTURE**®, my 2011 TEDxRainier talk, so he invited a group of friends over to watch it and he drew pictures of his dream: him shooting his first short film, then the initial screenings, the audience applauding, and he even drew himself accepting multiple awards for the film. Then he chose **3 BOLD STEPS** to activate the dream:

1. Write the script,

2. Start a Kickstarter campaign to crowd-source partial funding,

3. Assemble a film crew.

Over the following months he did just that. He carried out all three steps and, **BOOM**, one year later he was in Bali shooting his first film!

After his initial cut he started thinking, "**YOU KNOW, MAYBE THIS MOVIE ISN'T VERY GOOD, I DON'T HAVE NEARLY ENOUGH MONEY TO FINISH THE MOVIE AND I NEVER SHOULD HAVE QUIT MY JOB!**" On and on raged his internal critic. Mike panicked and eventually was paralyzed by his doubt. It was at this point that he sent me an email telling me that he'd felt like his **3 BOLD STEPS** had taken him exactly where he'd dreamed of going, but now…well…he was stuck. Nothing was happening the way it should. Was he on the brink of failure?

I wrote back, encouraging him to keep on going and assuring him that eventually he'd find his way if he didn't lose faith in the desire that fueled his dream. I suggested he go back to that original drawing and "double click" on some of the images on the future state side, using his imagination to reboot the strong desire that got him to make that film in the first place.

I was speaking to myself as well as to him. **I FACE THE SAME DOUBTS** when I feel lost or my work slows down unexpectedly. One of the tricks I use to remind myself to keep going is to remember this tip: as a cyclist exploring a new city, I know that whenever I feel lost, if I just keep pedaling a little farther, eventually I find my way. These days, when I'm on my bike or working on something I really want to have happen and I start to worry, I gently remind myself that if I wait and pedal just a little longer, the way will become clear and I'll find that I am right on track. I shared some of this with Mike and he listened quietly.

Next time I heard from Mike, he told me something amazing. His film, **MADE IN BALI**, had been screened at the Cannes Film Festival and 25 other festivals, and had won multiple awards in numerous countries! Yes! He was busy preparing to shoot his first feature film. His desire and sustained attention to his dream worked hand-in-hand to deliver to him (on a silver platter) that desired new reality he'd longed for.

Lots of people spend hours longing for something to occur and asking themselves, "**WHY IS NOTHING CHANGING?**" Unleashing the full capacity of your Creative Genius takes belief and determination, fueled by desire: Einstein wore a hole in the floor pacing in a circle in meditation while running his thought experiments! Bestselling author Elizabeth Gilbert still forces herself to her desk every day to face the blank page and start to write. Former first lady Michelle Obama in her book **BECOMING**, wrote about getting up at 4:30 AM to work out before her kids woke up and her long busy days began. Tour de France competitors train in every kind of weather, drilling over and again on the same routes, preparing themselves for anything and everything. The desire is the spark that keeps you going when you know you must put your nose to the grindstone and get back to work.

It helps to remember that, when you feel stuck, you naturally get lulled back into old subconscious patterns of thinking and operating. These patterns are like old, outdated movies that feature a version of you from your past, often as you were at age 15 (or younger). When you train yourself to tap into your imagination and rekindle the desire that initially kickstarted you on your way, you will find creative ways to remain focused and immune to doubt.

Of course, staying focused isn't easy. Everyday life is full of distractions — social media, email, text messages, phone calls, the flow of people around you — all trying to get your attention. Without constant motivation, it's easy to lose your desire and shift your focus to other things. If you aren't careful, your dream can easily get swept away into that infinite sea of distractions.

CLAIMING CREATIVE GENIUS YOU REQUIRES CONSISTENT ATTENTION AND LOTS OF CREATIVE PROBLEM SOLVING AND HARD WORK.

LOVE — THE ESSENTIAL ELEMENT

Desire and love combined tap into **CREATIVE GENIUS YOU**. Love is the glue that connects all of us to everything we do and touch, to our universe and the people we meet, and to all living things around us. When the interest or passion for something is lagging, life requires you to make a shift — to do something to help yourself move forward or you will, by nature, regress backwards.

Love is the powerful energetic field that is in and around us. Like water, love is buoyant and will lift you from the doldrums. Often you and I close our hearts to love, because of our fear. The simplest way to make a shift out of feeling like you are a mouse running along in the wheel of life but not going anywhere, is to find a way to open your heart and reconnect with the energetic, ever-present pull of love.

WHENEVER I FEEL LIKE I AM "LOVELESS" I FIND A WAY TO GIVE. GIVING UNLOCKS YOUR HEART ALLOWING LOVE TO ENTER IT.

Once when I was young, I told one of my parents' friends that I wanted to be an actor when I grew up. I'll never forget what she said, **"WELL, THAT'S GOING TO BE A TOUGH LIFE! YOU BETTER THINK LONG AND HARD IF YOU REALLY WANT THAT."** I'm happy to say that her response did nothing to quell my desire to perform. Now I see that she was probably trying to warn me about the challenges many actors do face — constant rejection, hundreds of auditions and long, torturous periods of wondering, **"WILL THIS EVER HAPPEN?"**

It's true that even with persistence and a good amount of talent, an actor may never get a break that results in a fantastic role and public recognition. Even if they do, it can sometimes be short-lived. Just to land the part and sustain the role requires even more introspection and hard work than people can imagine.

In an interview with two actors from the NBC hit drama, **GRIMM**, the interviewer asked them about the kind of work it took to be good at their craft. Both reflected on the immense amount of time, usually working alone, that was required to unwrap the motivations behind their characters. They confessed that it wasn't for the faint of heart and not the kind of challenge they had originally anticipated as actors. Challenges are inherent to any career choice, which means you must guide your brain to keep motivated, so that desire for success will push you forward to achieve your goals.

As an actor myself, I found I couldn't tolerate the rejection that was the given in a traditional acting career, so I decided to create and perform my own material. This proved more satisfying and gave me infinitely more freedom with the kinds of stories, inspirational messages and format of my work. I knew I wanted to be an actor — that part was non-negotiable — but **WHAT I HAD TO DO WAS DISCOVER HOW TO DO THIS IN MY OWN WAY**, and that required that I let myself dream about what might be possible. Instead of settling for what passed for conventional wisdom about how to be an actor, I let myself create something unique to me.

Remembering that you are unique and who you are and what you do is the gift you were meant to bring to the world will help you keep going through multiple career shifts and difficult client work or dynamics. It will draw in the kinds of experiences that you need next, so you can continue to evolve and grow. If you proceed with a growth mindset, you operate from a space where all the experiences you have happen for you rather than to you.

ANY PROCESS THAT YOU FIND CHALLENGING IS THERE FOR YOU TO PRESS THE RESET BUTTON, IMAGINE ALL THE POSSIBLE WAYS THROUGH IT OR AROUND IT, THEN LET YOUR INTUITION GUIDE YOU TO THE ONE ACTION YOU CAN TAKE RIGHT NOW.

Then, when you go and do something right away, **BOOM!** You will reboot your desire to keep going.

Once you allow yourself to dream up the world you want to live in, and explore the essential heart of your dream, your desire also generates a deep and powerful force of attraction. With the window of opportunity wide open, and attention tuned in to your vision of what is possible, any small and actual success will drop a hit of dopamine into your brain to increase your confidence.

If you are ready, you can channel this surge into immediate action to take even bigger risks that can move you closer to your goal, faster. **CONFIDENCE IS THE BIPRODUCT OF PRIOR PERFORMANCE** says Dr. Benjamin Hardy, author of **PERSONALITY ISN'T PERMANENT**:

> YOUR PERSPECTIVE OF YOUR FUTURE AND YOUR PAST IS BASED ON WHAT YOU REALLY BELIEVE. YOU CAN FAKE POSITIVE AND POWERFUL BELIEFS IN THE SHORT-TERM. BUT WHAT YOU REALLY BELIEVE IS MORE CONSISTENT WITH YOUR RECENT PAST AND CURRENT SITUATION.

Success builds upon itself and when you take a risk and successfully achieve a goal, the bigger the better, you will have the confidence to move mountains.

REJECTION AND ROADBLOCKS

No matter your level of self-confidence you will hit roadblocks and rejection. These are big challenges and, at the same time, opportunities to expand your belief in yourself and ability to persevere. They can also be a litmus test for whether your goals are just a fantasy or an actual dream that you are ready to bring to life. After all, if the first setback you face has you saying to yourself, "**WELL, I DIDN'T REALLY WANT IT ANYWAY**..." that suggests this wasn't a true dream.

I wrote, dreamed and drew dozens of pictures of myself on stage as a speaker long before any call came inviting me to speak. Even without any outward signs, I continued to dream and draw images of the reality I wanted to create. Then suddenly **I REALIZED THERE WAS A BIG MISSING PIECE IN MY PLAN**. I was never going to be invited to act out my dream when no one knew who I was or what I had to say.

CONCRETE ACTION IS REQUIRED for you to put yourself out there where you and your products and services can be found. You may have to do hours of pro bono work to prove your worth. You may have to learn marketing, test your products or write a book to gain credibility. It's long hours and dogged work that moves you step-by-step towards your goal. But holding that mental model of yourself in that desired future will help shift your perception and behavior in fundamental ways.

Recently my wife Julie and I were driving through Oregon when we passed a sign on the freeway for the Monarch Hotel. Julie turned to me and asked, **"WASN'T THAT WHERE YOU GAVE YOUR FIRST TALK TO A GROUP OF CHIROPRACTORS?"** I was suddenly reminded of that time where I took one of my first steps towards becoming a keynote speaker. Interesting that my career was transformed at a hotel named after a butterfly, the timeless symbol of transformation. I had often thought of these magnificent butterflies as a metaphor for the personal change that occurs when our perspective shifts, often when it seems that nothing is happening the way we think it should. That talk literally changed how I perceived who I was and why I was here.

After my talk to the chiropractors, people rushed the stage (which really was just the front of the room, but it makes it sound more glamorous!) and I received lots of positive feedback and encouragement. My experience that day convinced me that I had what it took to inspire and motivate an audience. It marked the beginning of a new cycle for my wife and I as well. We had just moved to the Pacific Northwest after living in sunny Denver for many years. We struggled to adjust to the perpetual rain and cloudy skies. We wondered why we had left the familiar cocoon of our former lives to live in this dreary landscape where things seemed so hard. As a result of the talk and the feedback I received, we both felt encouraged to carry on with our commitment to our dreams. Like the monarchs, we emerged with a new perspective about our lives and where we were headed.

During the initial stages of coming out of your cocoon you may feel like a fragile butterfly just getting used to its wings. Like a butterfly, you can't emerge too quickly, or you won't be fully developed and ready for your new life. You must develop the strength in your wings as you learn all you can about the elements of your dream and the steps you must take to get there. Remember that desire is the fuel that powers your drive. Learning everything you can about what your next step entails and then expanding your abilities to grow into who you need to become is part of the unfolding.

Self-reflection and personal growth are key contributors to your ability to handle your success when you manifest your goal. Obstacles are to be expected, so when you encounter them, ask yourself, "**WHAT MORE CAN I LEARN ABOUT MY DREAM?**" Read inspiring articles or listen to podcasts or TED talks to fuel your belief that it will occur. This will help you find new solutions while you remind yourself this is your vision, to continue to be patient and keep working: it will happen. Positive self-talk helps you rekindle that desire and every risk you take will help you grow.

A MIND
THAT IS STRETCHED
BY HAVING
A NEW EXPERIENCE
CAN NEVER GO BACK
TO ITS FORMER
DIMENSION

OLIVER WENDELL HOLMES, JR

THE FOCUS OF LOVE

While desire has been defined as the act of strongly wishing or wanting something, it is much more than that. It also includes love and attachment, which harnesses your attention and directs your focus like nothing else.

Have your ever met someone who took your breath away? Have you ever fallen completely in love with someone? It is a sensation that resonates through every cell in your body. That kind of desire has the power to focus your attention and give you the drive to get what you want. What you experience when this happens is a blast of chemistry: the racing heart, the sleepless nights, all of it caused by three powerful neurochemicals: norepinephrine, dopamine and phenylethylamine. The neurotransmitters of love.

Active visualization is a direct way to uncover and upgrade your systemic thinking. By focusing on the object of your desire, turning your attention to something you are fascinated with, **YOU IMBUE IT WITH LOVE**. As you explore it using your imagination, the synapses in your brain fire again and again, merging new concepts with your history, weaving a tapestry of strategies leading to your desired goal.

These patterns, with applied focus and attention, begin to shape themselves in such a way that they mirror anything you are visualizing in your mind's eye. When you do this, it's as if you are creating your own private force field. Whether you are aware of it or not, attention and repeated focus on something (positive or negative), creates an environment that makes it possible for that idea, feeling or thought to take root.

History reminds us that the athletes who use powerful imagery to help regain their focus win Olympic gold. They combine this method with rigorous physical training to achieve success. That ongoing rehearsal cements the belief that they will win into their minds.

YOUR GOAL IS TO IDENTIFY HOW YOU CAN HARNESS YOUR DESIRE AND CHANNEL IT INTO CONSISTENT ACTION TO ACHIEVE YOUR GOALS.

Bringing desire into the process of envisioning your next step will fill a black and white outline of your future with vibrant color. For over twenty years, I have worked with individuals and groups to create images that depict their dreams for the future.

WHAT I HAVE SEEN OVER AND OVER IS THAT THE MOST SUCCESSFUL PEOPLE COMBINE PICTURES OF A POSITIVE FUTURE, FILL IT WITH THEIR DESIRE FOR SUCCESS AND TAKE SMALL, BUT CONSISTENT STEPS UNTIL THEY ACHIEVE THEIR GOALS.

BECOMING A ROLE MODEL FOR OTHERS

Desire reboots and inspires you and those with whom you are co-creating to accelerate achievement. It aligns your brain chemistry to move you in the direction you have chosen. Like rocket fuel, desire is stored potential waiting to be set on fire. It's this blast of energy that propels you forward, busting through obstacles and challenges to reach that star. It is the force behind every aspect of you and life.

When you or those around you are facing new challenges (a pandemic for example) in the process of working towards what you want, simply start your meeting or your day by asking everyone to imagine themselves living their desired state, achieving their goals, as if that life is happening right now. Yes, there are challenges, but focusing on your challenges only brings more of them to you. Focusing on the positive will fill you with new energy to get through the tough days.

If you let it, desire can also work like a balm. It can soothe your nerves and then surprise and ignite you. Think about people in the world who inspire you and surround yourself with pictures of these people who touch and move you, whether it is a leader or a sports figure or a mentor. Even watching an inspiring movie can ignite a stack of kindling inside that sets alight your desire to be your best and bring more of your talents out to the world.

There's no secret in using what in business they call a "future pull" to help you shift your focus towards the new. The only secret is that you are made of desire, formed from desire, and exude through your attention one thing: desire, which is pure and simple love.

ANY SHIFT TOWARDS THAT WHICH YOU LOVE, OR THAT WHICH YOU WANT TO EXPERIENCE, IS YOU ACTIVELY USING THE DESIRE COMPONENT OF THE CREATIVE GENIUS EQUATION.

SEEKING TO SERVE

When you choose to bring your biggest and best self forward to handle a challenge or step up your game, you actively model for other people how to step into their best selves. Knowing that what you do and say in the world matters, knowingly becoming a role model — not from a place of ego but from a place of intuition — this is true service to others. The universe runs on this law of "**TO GET LOVE YOU MUST GIVE LOVE,**" every spiritual leader speaks about this. This kind of desire, to serve life, has been with you since you were born. It's your constant companion and will nurture you through anything if you let it.

IT STARTS BY KNOWING YOU BELONG TO THIS COSMIC FIELD WE LIVE IN, BECAUSE YOU ARE MADE FROM IT. YOU ARE LOVED AND BEAUTIFUL BECAUSE THE WORLD IS MADE UP OF A FORCE FIELD OF ENERGETIC LOVE.

Loving yourself is the essential ingredient in the recipe for a successful life or business. I'm not talking about self-love in terms of ego but in a reverent one. You exist because this universe, this energy, this force field, this whatever-you-want-to-call-it made you. Once you accept this concept, you open the door into the greater mysteries of life.

I wanted to call my first book **THE MAGIC OF CHANGE** because life is magical: how you and I are created and how our bodies, when left to themselves, will heal and grow and expand with our desire to learn more and expand our consciousness. You and I float in this sea of desire. The more you give love, the more you get love.

HOW CAN THIS CONCEPT HELP YOU PROBLEM SOLVE? That's the petri dish we are experimenting with in the **CREATIVE GENIUS EQUATION** in this element called **DESIRE**.

When you align your desire to a universal purpose for the good of the whole, then your solution, that vision for your life or your product or team, becomes a gift to others. That shift in awareness from **"ME"** to **"WE"** is what sparks the innovative current. Envision the best, choose the right direction to start, fill it with love and then surrender it up into the force field that you and I are made of. Then step forward and each day take another step and another, doing small things until you have stepped into that vision.

During COVID-19, the social app Clubhouse was created. It is an intimate space to help all of us learn and grow. People of all kinds share advice to grow a business or overcome mental health challenges or any other form of wisdom they are willing to share. It's often referred to as "**POURING INTO YOU**" love and generosity, information and education so that everyone who asks a question or is invited on stage is supported by the moderators on the panel. This selfless love for all humanity is what we yearn for. The reciprocity of giving and receiving is what helps everyone grow together.

As things begin to take shape, let your love and appreciation for everything that's coming your way expand through gratitude and let that gratitude open your heart. **DESIRE** is all about love and, no matter what you want, it will happen. **IT MAY SHOW UP IN A FORM THAT, AT FIRST, YOU DO NOT RECOGNIZE**.

Everything is here to shape and refine you so that you know at your core that deeper purpose for why you are here.

QUICK RECAP BEFORE WE MOVE ON

1. We all have desires and when what you desire is different than who you currently believe yourself to be, you create dissonance.

2. Desire signals your RAS which searches out examples for your new future self.

3. You can tap into your true desires by imagining a positive future that electrifies you and then take small consistent actions to achieve it.

4. Achieving your desires takes belief and determination despite consistent obstacles.

5. Serving others is a secret key to refueling your desire. Love out = love in.

EXERCISE: APPLIED EXPERIMENT — SIMPLY GIVE LOVE

FEELING CHALLENGED?

Find a way to make a list, note and appreciate the challenge for all the things it is helping you learn.

Send love to your environment, to all things big and small that support you: your house or apartment; the food you eat; the people you live near; those that serve you without your awareness.

Thank them by drawing a picture of gratitude and letting that love fill you and ripple out to everything and everyone you touch. Your love matters more than you can ever know.

5. DRIVE

SWEAT EQUITY

If desire is the driving force, then **"SWEAT EQUITY"** is your investment in your dream. It's the day-to-day action needed to achieve your goals and keep things moving towards them. It's also the process of continually learning what it takes to achieve mastery at your craft. It's late nights spent at your computer or writing in a notebook, it's that coding sprint, cycling that extra twenty miles or checking

THE TRICK TO CREATIVITY,
IF THERE IS A SINGLE
USEFUL THING
TO SAY ABOUT IT,
IS TO IDENTIFY
YOUR OWN PECULIAR TALENT
AND THEN
TO SETTLE DOWN
TO WORK WITH IT
FOR A GOOD LONG TIME.

DENISE SHEKERJIAN,
SOUL OF A WORD

details one more time. These all help you hone your skills and push yourself to connect your inspiration, desire and vision to something tangible. All this effort helps you form and reform your image of that future-you living your new life. And it's that image that will keep you going through long days engaged in the less-than-glamorous business of sweat equity. **THINK OF DRIVE AS ALL THE SMALL ACTIONS YOU TAKE TO HELP YOU CROSS OVER THE CHASM OF THE NOW TO THE NEW.**

Your willingness to invest in your dream gives you the commitment needed to go back to the drawing board repeatedly, with curiosity, as you try to understand what didn't work and uncover new ideas for what will.

Recently, I was watching the Tour de France and there was a person on a tightrope over this vast, expansive canyon. Yes, he had a guide-wire attached but he was out there a long, long way, just walking, one foot in front of the other. The commentators were saying things like, "**WOW! THAT'S A LONG WAY OUT THERE WITH JUST A CABLE HOLDING YOU IN PLACE.**"

That's **YOU** out there, facing your fear and putting one foot in front of the other.

SWEEPING THE PATH CLEAR TO CREATIVE GENIUS YOU

Many people feel like they get lost when their path seems blocked by resistance — from others, from external factors or from their own doubts, denial and fears — which keeps them from moving forward. But resistance is actually a powerful tool. It can help you build greater resolve or it can indicate that you might be out of alignment with the new direction you are taking.

Here is where you can tap into the information within you that knows exactly what needs to change and where to direct your efforts to bring about the change you are working on. Every time you listen to your intuition, you'll gain more clarity and more confidence in your ability to hear those nudges better. Then you'll find the drive you need to take action.

Once I worked with a senior executive who, after a conference, asked if I could do a mapping session for him. He felt it would be a good way to see what might be next in his future.

The CEO position in his company was going to be opening soon and he anticipated stepping in to fill that role. Naturally there would be a lengthy public interview process, outside search and all, but he believed he was a shoe-in. He kept reassuring me that he definitely felt okay either way, whether he got the job or not. If he didn't, he'd have the complete freedom to start a new career, the elements of which showed up quite clearly in the picture I drew for him.

A few months later, I sent him an email asking how things were going, fully anticipating that, by this time, he would have recognized the signs of freedom in his map. I was sure he would have quit his job and embarked on some new endeavor, maybe working for himself or being part of a different enterprise.

I was surprised when he told me he was still there, working in his same role and hating it. He told me that the search firm came in and they did something unexpected. They were hard-nosed and mean; everyone felt a little beat up afterwards. It had bruised his courage, and in the end he hadn't got the job. Then he mentioned how sick he was from working there and how he'd developed a debilitating illness.

"HMMM," I wondered out loud to him. "HOW LINKED ARE THOSE TWO THINGS?" He brushed it off and started to re-emphasize how much he wanted the new CEO to be successful. Then he stopped himself and said to me, "MAYBE IT ISN'T SUCH A GOOD IDEA, THIS JOB. MAYBE IT WON'T LEAD ME TO THE FREEDOM I WANT." Freedom was a big piece of the right side of his visual map.

I asked how he was using the map today, was he imagining it and using the images and words on the right side in the Desired New

Reality to help give him courage and more clarity. He confessed that he'd not really put his map somewhere he could look at it every day. It had been too much, he said. **HE DIDN'T WANT IT TO HAPPEN THAT FAST**.

This is a typical response when we have a fear or carry a burden of responsibilities and can't figure out how we will manage without the hated 9-5. We put our dream away; we shove it back into a drawer or the back of a closet.

THE GREAT THING ABOUT LIFE THOUGH, IS THAT EVERY-THING IS A CHOICE.

You might get insight and uncover a new level of truth when drawing your future, then decide to put it off. No harm, no foul — your Creative Genius is always there offering new information. The drive comes when you remain curious, asking yourself, "**WAS GETTING SICK WHILE WORKING AT THAT COMPANY SIMPLY RANDOM?**" Maybe, but research shows good health and happiness are intrinsically linked. The law of change dictates that if you're not happy, life will find a way to shift you out of where you are and into something new. Unexpected disruption occurs in the current state if you stay too long and know you don't want to be there, no matter how far back in the drawer your picture of the future is. Eventually your Creative Genius will force you out of your comfort zone and into the new world you have been fantasizing about. The question to ask is, do you want to drive that change or do you want to leave it until ill-health or some other outside driver takes hold of the wheel and forces you there?

What you imagine, even as a passing thought, becomes a road sign for your attention. 33% of your brain is automated, but 66% is programmable. You can harness your thoughts and point them towards the outcomes you desire. It's up to you, however, to stay awake while driving or you can miss all the off-ramps or on-ramps to the myriad of possibilities that exist in every moment.

FINE TUNE YOUR CREATIVE GENIUS WITH A PICTURE

Road signs are everywhere, so allowing yourself to simmer that vision on the stovetop of your imagination will help you gain clarity on any questions you have and let new ideas bubble to the surface. One way to get clear is to draw out what you want to experience when you have changed your life, whether it is specific to one area of your life or to the entire picture of how things are going.

In studies that were done to help people save for their retirement, they tested the efficacy of people drawing a picture of themselves as an older person to help build their empathy for, and desire to save for, that part of themselves. When you have an outer picture of that internal dream, it helps remind you what you are working for. For this reason, I go back to the **DRAW YOUR FUTURE**® process again and again to help anyone when they feel stuck.

When you draw it all out, you get that awesome snapshot of what really is occurring. That brings a deeper level of clarity so you can begin to work on taking concrete action. You won't hurt your vision by revisiting it or redrawing a map to focus on a specific piece. The map is a reflective portal and your Creative Genius will use it to speak to you. You may have other ways to help you know what you can do, so trust what you intuitively receive to help you get clear.

WHAT IF MY DREAM COMES TRUE?

Drive also makes you strong enough to withstand the response that sometimes comes with success. Pop icon Justin Bieber is a perfect example of someone who rocketed to stardom as a child with a great support system but then struggled to handle the reality of worldwide fame. His first response was to act out with bad behavior.

Then he realized he was probably going to have to figure out how to survive in the limelight and he slowly matured in his thinking and learned to live there. This motivated him to get back on track and do the work needed to find his own inner compass.

While you may not be working towards that kind of fame and fortune, it is possible that achieving your dreams may dramatically change who you are in the world and your relationships with people who think they know you. The new you may catch them by surprise and trigger a whole range of emotions in them such as an envy, jealousy and confusion.

At the same time, you may struggle to adjust to a life that isn't oriented around struggle and doubt and live in a world that isn't what you are used to. Just remind yourself that these are growing pains that are pivotal to your ability to embrace your new life.

THE TWO ELEMENTS THAT MUST WORK HAND IN HAND TO MOVE YOU FORWARD ARE YOUR WILLINGNESS TO INVEST YOUR SWEAT EQUITY, AND CONTINUOUS FUELING OF YOUR DRIVE.

GAINING TRACTION

There may be times when you feel stuck with your wheels spinning. Knowing you want to get some traction is a great first step but then what do you do next? Where should you expend your energy?

Here you can really start to apply the **CREATIVE GENIUS EQUATION** to level up your results when you feel stuck.

First, work with your imagination by creating pictures, reviewing anything you have written about what you want, and then spend time daydreaming what it will feel like to have achieved your goals.

Next, get concrete. Grab some Post-its® and write a task on each note — all the tasks, big and small, that you believe it will take to get there.

BEFORE YOU GET OVERWHELMED, create a way for your intuition to guide you as you prioritize the tasks, putting them into a matrix of boxes — for impact and effort — starting with 1 for the least important and increasing to 5 for the ones that are most important.

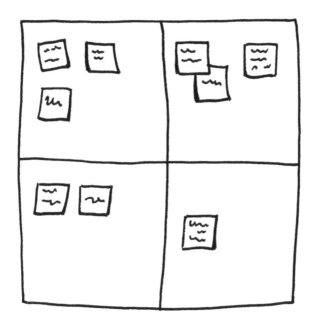

Once you have the matrix of your tasks, and you've assigned each task a number that indicates what level of priority you believe it should be, let this all-sink in. Close your eyes. Imagine yourself doing the task that has surfaced as a priority from your task matrix. Let yourself feel what it will be like to have accomplished it. The brain rewards you with a dopamine rush for your anticipation of completing a task as much as when you actually complete it. This exercise can be repeated with as many of the high priority tasks on your list as you like. Active engagement and dialogue with yourself to understand each task helps you clarify what help you need with these goals or the parts that are still unclear to you. Do this as often as you can.

Then, before you fall asleep at night, grab your journal, and write down all the big and small steps you took that day to move you closer to your vision. **EXPRESS GRATITUDE FOR EACH LITTLE AND BIG THING THAT HAPPENED**. Then set some goals for the following day. All of this keeps you motivated and focused so that you continue to inspire yourself to achieve your goals.

OPTIMIZE YOUR DRIVE BY MAPPING YOUR PLAN AND REVIEWING YOUR PROGRESS

Now optimize that plan of yours. These are the common components that lead to goal achievement:

1. **BELIEF**. Have absolute belief that you will achieve what you act on.

2. **VISION**. Create a detailed picture of your goal. Nothing fancy, just a sketch with all the elements of what you envision.

3. **PURPOSE**. Why is your goal important? Make a list of all the reasons you want it.

4. **PLAN OF ACTION**. Create a roadmap plan with specific, measurable, actionable and timebound goals.

5. **COMMIT**. Sign your work as a sign of commitment.

Creating a short-term plan focused on a few actions every week might be all you need. Put up some paper or use a white board to capture your ideas. In their book **GAME STORMING**, Sunni Brown and Dave Gray outline how to do a graphic game plan, and I renamed this the **"RAPID ROADMAP."** Put your goals for the week down the right side of the piece of paper and then map your timeline for the week and the small actions you will take to get there.

Don't be tempted to skip over this step. **THE ONLY SUPERHERO THAT WILL BRING THIS DREAM TO YOUR DOORSTEP IS YOU.** The time you take to plan now, even down to what time of day you will work on which action, these are the things that will take you across the finish line.

> A BENEFIT TO DOING THE DETAILED WORK ON YOUR PLAN IS IT WILL HELP YOU DISCOVER WHAT YOU NEED TO RESEARCH AND INVESTIGATE, OR DELEGATE, SO YOU CAN FOCUS ON THE RIGHT THINGS FOR YOUR GOALS.

Your ability to set big goals for yourself and attach aggressive, even outrageous timelines to those goals will force you to take bigger risks. Confidence is the byproduct of prior performance.

With your eye on that big North Star goal, everything that happens, which might seem weirdly tangential, will be part of a bigger plan, perhaps leading you to meet up with someone who will open the doors for you to that big break you longed for. Keep your focus on your goal, reminding yourself that each step is an integral part of your journey. You may not know where it's leading but if you remain focused you will glean every possible drop from the experience. This may mean that it's actually not a person that helps you step into your next chapter but in fact a deeper insight you gain, using your intuition as a guide.

GIVE YOUR DRIVE A TEAM

While in the **DRIVE** part of the **CREATIVE GENIUS EQUATION**, you may discover that your amazingly thorough and thoughtful action plan requires skills you personally don't have. If this is the case, one option is to take the time needed to develop a skill, such as how to read and understand a profit and loss statement or build a sales funnel. If the thought of doing this makes your heart rate go through the roof or you feel compelled to take a long nap, consider getting help by building a team.

If you are on a budget that doesn't cover this kind of expenditure, get creative. Can you swap services or courses with someone who could use your skill set? Even if you find a way to arrange support for your vision, remember that you are the person who is ultimately responsible for the heavy lifting, keeping the flow going, checking and rechecking details, and keeping sight of your goals. Day-to-day tasks may not feel very glamorous but each one is an act of commitment, a gesture signaling your belief in yourself and your dream.

During COVID, many business owners accustomed to delivering their services in person were forced to sell their services online. Many weren't sure how to market those products or services online and the online space was already packed with other people's offers. For those entrepreneurs willing to roll up their sleeves and figure out how to increase their business visibility, they were able to pivot to the online space and continue to serve their clients virtually.

EXTERNAL CHANGE LIKE THE ONE WE ALL EXPERIENCED WITH COVID REQUIRES COURAGE AND THE WILLINGNESS TO BE HUMBLE AND ADMIT IT'S TIME TO CHANGE HOW YOU DO THINGS AND THEN TO GET BUSY.

This is the kind of drive that change requires. Naturally you can hire people to help, but you need to know what you don't know and sometimes that means even if you have been in business for a long time, you must learn things you never even imagined nor necessarily wanted to, so you know what actions will make your business successful.

Galileo, a Creative Genius if there ever was one, believed that the synergy between sight and imagination, visual and conceptual, technique and creativity, creates the possibility for groundbreaking results. **LET'S PUT THIS CONCEPTUAL HOW-TO-SHIFT-YOUR-BUSINESS, YOUR HEALTH OR YOUR LIFE INTO THAT GALILEO TYPE ACCELERATOR.**

To help us see this together, I created this wall of notes, using an online coaching business as an example. Feel free to create your own wall of notes for yourself instead.

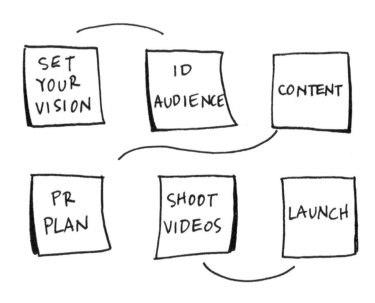

While looking at these words or images, ask yourself, **"WHAT DO I KNOW AND DON'T KNOW ABOUT HOW TO SCALE THIS NEW ONLINE BUSINESS, CHANGE MY HEALTH HABITS OR STEP INTO THAT FUTURE-ME?"** Add connections to what you see in front of you. Allow your intuition to help you identify what connections you should make, and which other people might benefit from your services or help you on your wellness journey or could be an accountability partner. **WHAT DO YOU BELIEVE YOU MUST DO TO GET FROM WHERE YOU ARE TO WHERE YOU DREAM OF BEING?**

If you're not sure which of these elements you've generated are necessary or important, make a list of all your actions, then imagine you have a total of 100 dollars, (or Euros, Pounds, or your country's money) to divide amongst these steps. Which step will you give the most money to? The ones you give the most money to in this **GAME STORMING** activity are the ones you consider your top priorities.

KEEP WORKING WITH THE CREATIVE GENIUS EQUATION TO REFINE YOUR NEXT STEPS, EVALUATE YOUR NETWORK CONNECTIONS AND REFINE YOUR ACTION STEPS. YOU CAN LEARN A LOT BY SIMPLY RUNNING A POSITIVE OUTCOME OVER AND OVER IN YOUR HEAD. YOUR CREATIVE GENIUS WILL DROP IN NEW IDEAS FOR YOU.

This iterative process will help you revise both what actions you take and (sometimes) your goals, based on what you are learning as you grow.

Now, to make it super concrete, map your actions into a visual timeline that begins today. Go do something right away, so you can tap that success button and refuel your motivation. Keep picturing yourself as that successful future you. What does it look and feel like? Remember to do this as if it is already happening.

TO-DO LISTS TEND TO BE LONG;
SUCCESS LISTS ARE SHORT.
ONE PULLS YOU IN ALL DIRECTIONS;
THE OTHER AIMS YOU
IN A SPECIFIC DIRECTION.
ONE IS A DISORGANIZED DIRECTORY, AND
THE OTHER IS AN ORGANIZED DIRECTIVE.
IF A LIST IS BUILT AROUND SUCCESS,
THEN THAT'S WHERE IT TAKES YOU.

GARY KELLER,
*THE ONE THING: THE SURPRISINGLY SIMPLE TRUTH
BEHIND EXTRAORDINARY RESULTS*

NOW IT'S YOUR TURN!

Take some time to complete this simple assessment. The result is going to be the starting point for your plan.

My idea:

What is my purpose?

What will success look like?

WHO NEEDS TO BE INVOLVED TO ACHIEVE THIS SUCCESSFULLY?

Skills I need to learn or hire for, including the type of person that can activate this part of my plan.

1.

2.

3.

Now let's drill down into a support team for you. In my **FLIP YOUR FEAR AND CRUSH THE VIRTUAL STAGE** I talk about five key roles that can help build a successful support team:

1. **MENTOR**: a mentor is someone who can coach you, introduce you to key people and guide you to projects or products that will set you up for success and ongoing learning. When you start to look for a mentor, remember to get to know them a little bit first so you find a someone who is

interested in helping you be successful. Set the stage by letting them know what you are looking for and invite them to tell you what they can offer you as a mentor. Mentorship is a two-way street, so you'll be bringing your awesomeness to their world too!

WHO CAN I CALL TO ASK IF THEY WILL MENTOR ME?

2. **PEER**: develop a relationship with one of your peers who is also aiming for a similar goal (maybe starting a business or working for a promotion). Michele Obama shares in her podcast how a peer in DC became one of her closest friends and how valuable that friendship was when she entered a room full of strangers and needed to know how to navigate it. A peer can help you sort through issues, cheer you on and offer advice. They may also offer a helping hand should you need it.

WHO WILL BE A PART OF MY CHEER SQUAD?

3. **CREATIVE PARTNER**: one of the greatest benefits to having a creative partner, someone who is just fun to noodle ideas with, is that they truly can **UP YOUR CREATIVE GENIUS**. Over the years I have built multiple relationships with creative partners, all of whom have helped me be successful. Find someone who you love to work with that will challenge you and encourage you, but always supports you.

WHICH CREATIVE PARTNERS CAN I CONNECT WITH?

4. **CONFIDANTE**: during this time, you need a confidante more than ever. A confidante might be your partner or a close friend, with whom you can share your big secrets and fears. They provide a listening ear but are not so much about giving you guidance as they are sharing the load with you in a two-way exchange.

WHO WILL BE MY CONFIDANTE?

5. **TECH GURU**: this is a must have in today's world. Someone who can fix your computer, open a program, install security, run your Zoom conferences for you, set up your online classes and so much more. You can find good people on Upwork. Try them for a week on something small and see how they do. You can also hire someone in your local area or invite your tech savvy daughter or son for help. I have found that it's easier if I paid them and they weren't my significant other. This way I can set up a schedule for them to meet their deliverables.

WHO CAN SOLVE ALL MY TECH PROBLEMS?

You can also set up an informal support group of peers. In my mentor-ship program, I see time and again how the entrepreneurs in the program bond together and support each other, inviting each other to beta groups or holding pep rallies or drawing sessions between our biweekly organized meetings. They use the elements of the Creative Genius to get support and rework their products together.

ARE YOU LETTING YOUR DRIVE BE DETOURED BY DOUBT?

When you are up against the wall and facing real challenges (like finding the money to pay the bills), you can lose heart and be tempted to abandon your desire for change. Even though you are paying attention and looking for inspiration, you may find yourself in a place where you start to think to yourself that this is not happening fast enough.

DOUBT STARTS TO UNDERMINE YOUR DRIVE UNTIL YOU FIND YOURSELF THINKING THAT WHATEVER YOU DID BEFORE WAS PROBABLY BETTER THAN THIS. WATCH OUT!

In that moment you must catch yourself and recognize that your brain is trying to revert to old patterns and a former you. While you do control your perceptions of the universe, your level of consciousness is limited (or expanded) by your beliefs.

What happens when hard work doesn't immediately show the results you hoped for? It's easy to start judging the situation or yourself and tell yourself what you should or shouldn't have done. You enter the old familiar, well-worn groove of responding in the exact ways that shaped your past. Then you will probably also embark on a marathon of negative self-talk, reassuring yourself that, **"THIS FEELS FAMILIAR. I'M COMFORTABLE HERE. I THINK I'LL JUST STAY HERE INSTEAD OF..."** Suddenly you start to lose steam until you come to a screeching stop.

Sound familiar? This backslide may continue for hours, days, sometimes even years, until you can **WREST YOURSELF OUT OF THE ABYSS AND REVIVE YOUR DESIRE FOR CHANGE.** No matter how much time you feel like you have lost, you can still reconnect with your drive, engage the clutch, put it in first gear and start to move forward again.

In almost every workshop I have led, when people get in touch with their dreams, someone will inevitably approach me to ask in a whisper, **"IS IT TOO LATE?"** My answer is always the same: **"NEVER, IT'S NEVER TOO LATE UNLESS YOU FEEL IT IS!"**

Whenever I feel overwhelmed or frustrated by the pace at which change is (or isn't) happening, I reboot my focus by reaching for a notebook or scrap of paper and I draw a picture of what's next — that new me, my new world, my 20-years-out self. This simple act helps me see beyond the current situation and reconnects me with what I know is possible.

In a recent study conducted by Dr. Hal Hershfield at UCLA in collaboration with the Consumer Protection Bureau, they measured the effectiveness of having people **DRAW YOUR FUTURE**® to help individuals connect with their future self. The study was created because almost 60% of the population isn't saving for their retirement. Hershfield's previous work identified that this was due to them not having a clear picture of their future self, complete with aging and retirement, to compel them to save money in the here and now.

We all have our own personal demons that stand between us and where we'd like to be in life. When we encounter them, we need to do something to redirect our thinking pattern away from the voices that tell us we don't deserve whatever we are striving for.

This is the perfect time to get practical and shift your perspective. Acknowledge what is going on, then do some intentional deep breathing. Try using a four-part breathing technique where you breathe in gently for four counts, hold four counts, out for four counts, hold for four counts. Sit down and do a few minutes of meditation, go for a walk or even do a few quick push-ups.

REMEMBER TO KEEP YOUR SELF-CRITIC FROM SABOTAGING YOU. YOU MIGHT EVEN NEED TO SET BOUNDARIES WITH OTHER PEOPLE WHO FEEL IT'S THEIR RIGHT TO DOUBT YOUR ABILITY TO DO THINGS DIFFERENTLY.

Refocusing takes as little as 10 seconds. You don't even have to close your eyes. Simply see yourself in your mind's eye doing the thing you want to do. Sometimes, despite having the best intentions to remain positive and focused, your fear worms its way in and harangues you with old, outdated memories. Stop the action to acknowledge your fear. Place your hand on the place you feel it in your body. Sometimes I will say out loud, **"ALRIGHT, I MUST BE AFRAID OF SOMETHING HERE."** Then, I find a way to open my heart, remind myself of something I love or recall someone who believes in me. When I feel connected to that love, I ask for a simple next step and let my inner hard drive reboot. Then I act immediately.

REPATTERN YOUR REACTION AND THEN HAVE A PLAN TO HELP YOU REBOOT

When you feel stuck, you might pick up the phone and call the friend who has the job you want and ask if there are any other openings. Or go out and replace that front flower bed because your goal is to sell your house and get a smaller condo downtown. Or knock on your landlord's door to ask if they might consider trading time for your rent if you commit to doing improvements on a regular basis. Or list ways to earn extra cash so you can hire that administrative assistant. Or stay with friends in town and Airbnb your home.

At the end of every day, make a list of all you are grateful for. Make sure to get enough sleep to have the energy to bring to your project. You can change and modify your energy. *Huffington Post* contributor, Stephenie Zamora, suggests these three simple ways: change your environment; change your location; change your mindset. Something as simple as changing the wallpaper on your phone or computer or sitting in a different chair will press that reset button inside of you.

LESSENING THE LIMITING BELIEFS

There you are enjoying the gloriosity (I think I made that word up, but isn't it fantastic?) of working on your unique, amazing, and powerful vision.

Unbeknownst to you, lurking in the shadows, just waiting until you have had too long of a day or eaten too much sugar or bumped into an ex, are those old thinking patterns that remind you that, "**YOU CAN'T DO THIS, YOU'RE NOT SMART ENOUGH, CUTE ENOUGH, DISCIPLINED ENOUGH**." Those outdated beliefs, that are often formed before the age of 15, are just waiting for you to let your guard down so they can attach to you like a dog with a bone and arrest your development.

"Now what?!" you exclaim and throw your arms up with an "**AAH!**"

Stay calm Superstar, you are equipped to reroute this pesky amygdala! But my thinking is, why do it in arears? Why not circumvent the old patterns and behaviors by getting in front of them, learning all about them so you can change them? They've been pestering you for years, grabbing your attention and derailing you. Why not take the time to give them some direct attention?

LIMITING BELIEFS

Ask yourself, "**WHAT BELIEFS DO I CURRENTLY HOLD ABOUT MYSELF OR THIS SITUATION THAT MAY STOP OR SLOW MY PROGRESS?**" Grab your pen and make a list. To help you jog your memory, common beliefs include things like, "**I DON'T KNOW ENOUGH,**" "**I'M NOT SMART ENOUGH,**" "**I'M TOO OLD,**" "**I DON'T HAVE ENOUGH TIME.**"

You might feel you aren't valuable, not loveable or not credible. Any of these ring true from your past? You probably recognize a few. Keep a running list of limiting beliefs somewhere and review them from time to time to give yourself a heads up when your drive is about to stall. While your focus should be firmly placed on the positive beliefs of achieving your goals, you are human, so you are bound to have triggers that send you on a self-deprecating detour. Lift your level of awareness so you can reduce their ability to undermine your progress.

Another powerful way to shift your old beliefs is to stop the action and imagine yourself replacing it in your mind with the new belief.

PICTURE YOURSELF LIFTING OUT THE SQUIRMING SNAPPING DOUBT AND DROPPING IT INTO THE TRASH AND THEN PLACING SOMETHING POSITIVE INTO THE GAP.

Keep repeating that new belief to yourself. Doing this, you will re-pattern the way your brain works. You can also do this before you encounter a situation that you feel might trigger old beliefs.

Try repeating to yourself, "**I AM SMART, CREATIVE AND CAPABLE**," when going in for a job interview or, "**I AM ENOUGH**" when revisiting a situation where you have felt your self-esteem lagging.

Your brain is malleable and you can shift your brain patterns with a little work. In David Eagleman's book, **THE BRAIN**, he describes a study about "visual spatiality." Subjects were given goggles that reversed what they were looking at. Things that were on the right appeared to be on the left, things above them seemed to be below, and so on. When people used the goggles for the first time, they got nauseous and broke out in a nervous sweat. However, after a few days, their cognitive function adjusted to the new vantage point of right and left and their discomfort stopped. After two more days, their neurons had reconstructed the brain so that this spatial awareness was now the new normal.

EAGLEMAN'S STUDY DEMONSTRATES THAT THE BRAIN DOESN'T CARE ABOUT THE ACTUAL DETAILS OF THE INPUT; IT IS BUSY RECONFIGURING THINGS TO EFFICIENTLY ACHIEVE THE TASK AT HAND. IF YOUR BRAIN CAN RECONSTRUCT SPATIAL REALITY AFTER ONLY TWO WEEKS, WHAT ELSE IS IT CAPABLE OF RECONSTRUCTING?

The brain uses more than just vision to construct reality. When your brain is deprived of all sensory input (for example when in a sensory deprivation chamber), it will reconstruct reality and start making things up. Eagleman writes,

"IN FACT THE BRAIN GENERATES ITS OWN REALITY EVEN BEFORE IT RECEIVES INFORMATION COMING IN FROM THE EYES AND OTHER SENSES. THIS IS KNOWN AS THE INTERNAL MODEL."

Left to its own devices, your brain will start making stuff up, so it is critical that you direct it to construct the reality you want to live in, not the one you fear.

When you have a plan that includes a clear picture of the new you, the feelings you will experience in the new world and a plan of action to get you there, you have given your brain a roadmap. Now your brain recognizes, "OKAY THIS IS THE PATH WE ARE TAKING TO THAT GOAL." The faster you work to meet small goals, the more efficient you'll become in driving in the right direction. The more often you reinforce your goals with images, feelings, and positive beliefs the deeper you embed them into the workings of your brain.

Jenna wrote to me about the picture of the future she drew and subsequently experienced.

"AFTER ATTENDING ONE OF YOUR KEYNOTES, I ADMIT I WAS SCEPTICAL ABOUT THE PROCESS. DID IT REALLY WORK? I WAS OPEN TO TRYING THE EXPERIMENT. SO, I DREW ON THE RIGHT SIDE OF MY MAP MY HUSBAND COOKING ME DINNER — SOMETHING I WANTED BUT RARELY EXPERIENCED. WITHOUT SAYING A WORD TO ANYONE ABOUT MY IMAGINED REALITY, I CAME HOME TWO NIGHTS LATER TO FIND MY HUSBAND COOKING DINNER FOR ME.

"I THOUGHT, 'OH PERHAPS THAT WAS JUST A COINCIDENCE,' BUT IT WORKED TIME AND AGAIN WHEN I FOCUSED MY ATTENTION ON WHAT I REALLY WANTED, WROTE IT DOWN, DREW A PICTURE AND ASSUMED POSITIVE INTENT, THAT THIS WAS GOING TO HAPPEN. NOW THIS PROCESS IS FULLY INTEGRATED INTO MY EVERYDAY PLANNING."

By now I have impressed you with the neurological research which tells us that approximately one third of our brain function is automatic, while the rest is programmable. But it is iterative, too. Instead of using your senses to constantly recreate reality from scratch every moment, your brain adds new sensory information to a model it previously constructed from your past experiences. This updating, refining, and reconstructing is ongoing every minute of every day even though you are totally unaware of it.

You can see how this might be the underlying reason you sometimes experience circumstances and situations you know you wouldn't consciously choose. The amygdala, under stress, will do anything to solve a problem you are facing. Its default response is to follow a familiar pattern to give you a sense of completion and when you do, you get a hit of dopamine in your body.

On a chemical level your brain tells you it feels good to solve that problem and the quicker the better. Subsequently, it will drop in an old negative belief for why you didn't get the result you wanted: **"SEE YOU REALLY AREN'T THAT GOOD!"** it tells you. Job done, **BOOM!** Hit of dopamine. The good news is that when you understand how your brain works, you can direct it to solve the problem with new beliefs and positive patterns of thinking that support you achieving your goals and desires.

REMEMBER THAT LIST OF ALL THE LIMITING BELIEFS I ASKED YOU TO CREATE?

Look at each one and ask where they came from: memories that you have of what people said or how you felt when confronted with different life experiences or some other way you arrived at it. Then write a positive belief to replace the negative or limiting one.

Now, track yourself in your day and note what triggers the belief that might be holding you back. When the old way of thinking starts to play like a broken record, stop what you are doing and say or do something to break the cycle.

For example, say out loud (I find it helps to do it loudly), "**CHANGE!**" then repeat your positive belief to yourself. Next reward yourself in some way. "**YES, I DID IT! YAY!**" Activate your inner cheerleader to make this one stick!

ALL IN GOOD TIME

Sometimes change happens so fast we can hardly keep up. Have you ever wanted something to change and it happened so quickly that it really did feel like magic? Whenever this happens to me, I get super curious and ask, what made the difference? What was it that helped me accelerate the process?

When we were planning to move to Portland, Julie and I searched and searched (and searched some more) for a new home. It was an arduous task but finally we found the house we wanted. We worried the sale might not go through for all the reasons home buyers feel anxious when making such a big decision. To our surprise the loan was approved almost immediately and the sellers accepted our very first offer. In less than a month we were moving into our new home.

Everything had gone so smoothly that, frankly, it left our heads spinning! We were curious how this seemed to happen so quickly, when purchasing our first home in Seattle eight years earlier had seemed so difficult.

When we unpacked our experience, we found there were some key things we did when moving this time. Since we had been through this before we had all the paperwork sorted and our mortgage lender was superb: organized, helpful and friendly. That meant if anything else was needed, we were happy to comply. We also were not attached to the outcome. Naturally we wanted a great home but we both saw Portland as an adventure and agreed that we would just listen to our Creative Genius and trust that we would find a home in the perfect spot.

We had also made a drawing of the kind of home we were thinking about and a list of things we wanted in the home: lots of light, high ceilings, yard for the dogs, great neighbors..., and we kept that picture and shared it with our realtor, so she knew exactly what we were looking for. Each of these things added to the ease of sale.

I have noticed that when things are easy, we often say it was "**MEANT TO BE**." When things don't work out as we hoped, however, we shrug and say the exact opposite. But what if it's all meant to be? That every experience is there just for you? If you hold that belief, then it puts the onus on you to unravel the mystery of why things went in one direction instead of another. Clearly there is something to be learned when this happens. When things don't turn out as we'd imagined, we want to take time to reflect, to see if a course correction is needed, then, once realigned we can reactivate our desire, imagine the positive outcome and get back to work.

IF YOU SHIFT YOUR FOCUS TO PAY ATTENTION TO THE AMAZING THINGS THAT ARE OCCURRING RIGHT NOW, AS WELL AS THOSE THINGS THAT ARE NOT HAPPENING AS YOU HOPED THEY WOULD, YOU MAY DISCERN A PATTERN.

Not all big things happen in the time frame we hope they will. Sometimes small changes bring an even more profound movement within us. These subtle shifts help us step into the person we need to become to accept those bigger goals. Small steps add up to big steps. Small actions underlie each piece of the **CREATIVE GENIUS EQUATION**. Together they will help you achieve your outcome to the infinite degree.

USE SPIRITUAL EXERCISE TO TRAIN FOR THE FUTURE YOU

At first, driving a car is a really complicated, stressful experience: hand signals, traffic lights, speed limits, all those cars whizzing by you... Do you remember how it felt? Every intersection generated panic. After a while your brain created pattern memories of how to drive, allowing your neural pathways to provide you with automatic reactions, until it was seamless, instant and unconscious.

IT'S ASTOUNDING TO STOP AND THINK ABOUT HOW MANY THINGS YOUR BRAIN DOES AUTOMATICALLY!

While this function of the brain makes it possible to move through our days without having to fully concentrate on every little thing we do, the challenge is to be able to move out of this state when needed. One way is by altering your consciousness through meditation or other mindfulness practices.

One goal of meditation is to create a state of awareness in which your mind is calm and completely alert. When you meditate on a regular basis, several positive things happen. In the article, **THIS IS YOUR BRAIN ON MEDITATION**, Dr. Rebecca Gladding describes what happens to your brain.

"FIRST, THE STRONG, TIGHTLY HELD CONNECTION BETWEEN WHAT IS THE ME CENTER, SPECIFICALLY THE UNHEALTHY PARTS OF US THAT ARE CRITICAL AND THE BODILY SENSATION/FEAR CENTERS, BEGIN TO BREAK DOWN. AS THIS CONNECTION WITHERS, YOU WILL NO LONGER ASSUME THAT A BODILY SENSATION OR MOMENTARY FEELING OF FEAR MEANS SOMETHING IS WRONG WITH YOU OR THAT YOU ARE THE PROBLEM!"

Learn to shift your anxiety by simply taking a few deep breaths and becoming completely present. Out of that presence will often come an insight into something you need to know, learn or do. But spiritual exercise for you as soul is just like physical exercise for your body. It will increase your capacity to tap into and receive new ideas. It also can shift you beyond the constant chattering of your mind into a quiet alpha state where your sense of connection increases.

In a deeply meditative state, it's as if you are mentally awake as your body goes to sleep. Thomas Edison reportedly would get in a very relaxed meditative state while holding a few ball bearings in his hand. He wanted to stay in the place of being deeply relaxed, unhooked from the realm of thinking but not falling completely asleep. If he got too relaxed and started to fall asleep, he would drop the ball bearings, which would wake him up. He believed that in this state between being fully awake and sleeping, he was able to make more powerful connections and generate new concepts more easily.

When I'm developing new material for a course, client engagement or a talk for a keynote, I first sit in meditation to become deeply relaxed.

I imagine I am an observer in that arena and watch the audience or client group seated before me. Then I shift my perspective so that **I AM IN THE AUDIENCE, SITTING AMONGST THEM**, watching myself playing out that scene or giving the talk from stage. Meanwhile, I have a pen in my hand so that I can write down anything that occurs to me while watching the scene in my mind. By creating rapport between myself on stage and myself observing, I am able to assess various dimensions of my presentation. Without fail I am flooded with ideas that hadn't occurred to me before when I'd been thinking about the content directly.

Over time I have come to realize that I can use this same technique to solve any other challenge I am facing.

FOR EXAMPLE, IF I AM HAVING AN ISSUE WITH A CLIENT, I TAKE BOTH OF US INTO AN IMAGINARY CONFERENCE ROOM. I'LL ADD TO THAT ROOM A WISE FACILITATOR, MEDIATOR, MENTOR OR INNER TEACHER TO HELP GUIDE ME THROUGH THE CONVERSATION.

IN THIS INNER CONFERENCE ROOM, TALKING THROUGH THE ISSUE WITH AN IMAGINARY TRUSTED ADVISOR, INEVITABLY I GAIN INSIGHTS AS TO WHAT I CAN DO TO HELP RESOLVE THE SITUATION.

To get into a fully awake, daydream state you must silence your "critical observer" self. Who is our critical observer? That's the voice that keeps asking, "IS THIS REAL?" As far as your brain is concerned, it doesn't matter if it is real or not. If you can imagine it, it becomes a very real possible outcome.

After using this technique with a challenge I was having with a friend, I was amazed to find that I was in a completely different state of mind when I saw that friend again. I felt open and receptive and much more compassionate about their situation. It was almost as if the inner dialogue I'd imagined had occurred in the physical world. The brain's plasticity is impacted by both environment and experience. If we continually have disruption and angry inner dialogue, the brain forms patterns around that negativity but when we create a new, positive normal and begin to act on it, we step into that reality.

BLENDING BELIEF WITH DRIVE

While many of us think it's the outer drive that is the key to achieving our goals, it is both the alignment between the inner thoughts, feelings and behaviors coupled with action which accelerates our success. The capacity to change and be changed isn't limited to people who "have the time to daydream." It's available to all of us because our default is to daydream. If you ask anyone how they transformed their reality from a place where their basic needs were not met into something great, they will say, "**I BELIEVED IT WAS POSSIBLE AND I KEPT GOING**." Belief and action.

How does belief set reality? If we are genetically encoded to repeat or play out a pattern set in our brain, it is up to us to work to discover how we can sidestep or alter that plan. That means you must work to change your beliefs and you can through persistent practice. Anyone who's ever initiated, repeated and sustained something for an extended period — trained for a marathon, written a play or movie, built a business, learned to meditate — will tell you the most important part was discipline. Consistently showing up, practicing

THIS IS THE OTHER SECRET
THAT REAL ARTISTS KNOW,
AND WANNABE WRITERS DON'T.
WHEN WE SIT DOWN EACH DAY
AND DO OUR WORK,
POWER CONCENTRATES AROUND US.
THE MUSE TAKES NOTE OF OUR DEDICATION.
SHE APPROVES.
WE HAVE EARNED FAVOR IN HER SIGHT.
WHEN WE SIT DOWN AND WORK,
WE BECOME LIKE A MAGNETIZED ROD
THAT ATTRACTS IRON FILINGS.
IDEAS COME.
INSIGHTS ACCRETE.

STEVEN PRESSFIELD,
THE WAR OF ART:
BREAK THROUGH THE BLOCKS AND WIN
YOUR INNER CREATIVE BATTLES

your pitch, doing all those daily tasks… All success is linked to how much focus and attention you place on achieving your goal.

Repeatedly work the equation to help you create breakthrough in your results. Each part of it fuels and funds your "will to succeed" account. You are the common denominator to your own success. You are the one and only person who holds your dream with clarity and vision. **CREATIVE GENIUS YOU** is the one who can and will make it happen.

LET'S PUT A PLAN TO YOUR DRIVE — EXAMPLE

When you apply the process to setting a health goal and focusing your drive to achieve it, you first start by identifying what you want to be different. Maybe it's boosting your discipline to help you to stay or get into shape. Use your imagination to get clear on what you really want to change by imagining the body or goal fulfilled, like lifting a certain amount of weight or regaining some flexibility you have lost.

Now that you are clear on what you'd like to achieve, tap into your intuition to give you a sense about what part of how you currently take care of your health will help you get the best results. Fuel your desire by clarifying how much you want this change to happen.

WHAT WILL IT FEEL LIKE WHEN YOU HAVE DROPPED THOSE 10 POUNDS OR ADDED 10 POUNDS TO THE NUMBER OF WEIGHTS YOU CAN LIFT IN THE GYM?

Now add in the drive. Set in place a structure, schedule and process to achieve your goal.

Often when people start the action planning part, they start too aggressively: "I'M GOING TO GO RUNNING 6 DAYS A WEEK!" If you are accustomed to that kind of discipline and you are currently running 4 days a week, this goal might be easy to accomplish. However, if you have been sitting on your couch throughout fall and winter, the first time you strap on those running shoes and go out there, your legs are going to be dying and this will often send you right back to the couch, thinking, "GEEZ, I THINK I'D BETTER TAKE A REST. MAYBE I'LL START THAT RUNNING PROGRAM NEXT WEEK."

Instead, start with the idea that you'll run two days a week and maybe stretch or do yoga two days a week and check to see how that works. You may need to initially challenge yourself to get off the couch but each level of success will boost and reinforce your actions by giving you immediate gratification. "HEY, I DID IT!" hits that dopamine success button in your internal chemistry and keeps you motivated to do it again when it's raining outside.

Reassess and revise your plan to increase or decrease the amount of what you are doing to be realistic. This reassessing helps your brain to know you are in control and this goal will be achievable.

The second piece that supports efficacy is to do something towards the goal you have right now. Do not wait. Pick up the phone, get off the couch, overcome your fear posing as inertia, make the call, write in the journal. Open the savings account and put money in the bank. Once you have even minor success towards achieving your goal, the brain's natural chemistry will kick in to help you continue, but it needs to be fueled by the belief that you can do it and will take actions to get there. Take the time to align your beliefs with what you need to do and why. Here are some examples of how to do that:

1. Cut back to just 1 cup of coffee. **BELIEF: "COFFEE IS GREAT IN MODERATION FOR ME."**

2. Setting up the trainer. **BELIEF: "AS A CYCLIST, RIDING ON THE TRAINER INDOORS IS A GOOD THING WHEN IT'S TOO COLD TO GO OUTSIDE OR MY SCHEDULE IS TIGHT."**

3. Bring the smaller weights with you when you are taking your kids to the park, then use them. **BELIEF: "I CAN MAKE THE THINGS I NEED ACCESSIBLE, SO I CAN FOLLOW THROUGH WITH MY HEALTH GOALS."**

4. Take action towards your goal; then celebrate it. **BELIEF: "NEW THINGS HELP CREATE NEW NEURAL PATHWAYS**

WHICH ADDS TO MY FLEXIBILITY. CELEBRATION HELPS ME WANT TO DO IT AGAIN."

Any ordinary person can make extraordinary things happen. The sequence of events that lead you to take your next action step simply require that you navigate the inevitable disruptions you might face (like illness, a slow month in your business, or a feeling that there's something in what you are currently doing that needs to change). **"WE ARE KEPT FROM OUR GOAL NOT BY OBSTACLES, BUT BY A CLEAR PATH TO LESSER GOALS,"** Robert Brault reminds us. All your goals are important or interesting to you but some of them are lesser goals, even if you really want them.

If you live a lifetime without doing that thing you've been fantasizing about doing, you shut the door on **CREATIVE GENIUS YOU**. Continue to boost your drive and act on your intuitive nudges when they come, to keep moving forward; testing and trying, learning and growing, until you wake up one day and realize you are the person you dreamed about in a life you have created for yourself.

QUICK RECAP BEFORE WE MOVE ON

1. Ultimately, to achieve your goals, you need to take action. The desire you have will fuel your drive to take bold steps.

2. **IT IS NORMAL TO FEEL RESISTANCE TO CHANGE** and find taking action uncomfortable. You need to recognize the fear and doubt for what it is and tap into your Creative Genius and keep drawing pictures to keep moving forward. **START WITH SMALL ACTIONS** and build your confidence in your future as you make progress.

3. **DRIVE** requires practical, achievable actions to maintain it. For each goal, make a list of everything you could do and then narrow it down to what to do next.

4. **STAY CURIOUS**. As you take action, see what worked and what needs adjustment, so you keep your drive topped up. **IF THINGS DON'T GO TO PLAN**, look at what else you can try rather than doubting yourself and letting that sabotage you.

5. **SURROUND YOURSELF WITH OTHERS** in your team who have the skills you need to achieve your dreams.

EXERCISE: TELL OTHER PEOPLE

One of the simplest tools of them all for drive is to tell other people what you are planning.

By declaring what you are working on like "**I'M QUITTING SMOKING**," "**I'M GOING TO RUN A MARATHON**," "**I'M GOING TO START POSTING REELS ON INSTAGRAM EVERY WEEK**," those around you who love you will hold you to account and, because you know they know, you'll hold yourself to account too.

1. Pick an action you need to take or goal you want to achieve.

2. Create a list of 10 people or more (but not less) who you are going to tell about this.

3. Share your goal with them all and say you are telling them as you want their support to make sure you follow through on your promises.

6. OUTCOME$^\infty$

For the past five chapters, you have been learning to work with elements of the **CREATIVE GENIUS EQUATION:**

IMAGINATION x INTUITION + DESIRE x DRIVE.

Here is the most surprising part: when you continuously and consciously use all of yourself — find stillness long enough to listen to the quiet voice of your Creative Genius and marry that inner guidance with small consistent action — the results will be greater than you could ever imagine.

The results that you can envision are often based on only what our brain has seen, heard or previously experienced. But to truly tap into your potential, you must move beyond what the brain knows. You have no idea what the outcome∞ ("**OUTCOME TO THE INFINITE POWER**") is. To access that unknown, you need to consistently take risks in the here-and-now.

Your future self can be 20, 30, 50 years out there. Even now, when you envision the biggest goals possible, it is only from the "current-you" perspective. To tap into an infinite potential, you must build a pathway for that infinite potential to communicate with you.

THIS PART OF STEPPING INTO YOUR FUTURE IS MYSTERIOUS AND EXCITING BUT IT IS DETERMINED BY YOUR OPENNESS TO ACCEPT AND TAKE SCARY CHALLENGES; TO LEAP ACROSS THE CHASM TO THE FUTURE YOU THAT YOUR CREATIVE GENIUS IS POINTING TOWARDS.

Where you sometimes trip up is in your attachment to the exact image of what you imagine your life will be like in that future state. All those ideas are influenced by who you are now or who you used to be in the past. The brain's hippocampus is littered with outdated beliefs, so most of us continue to apply the same principles and behaviors that got us to where we are today.

The new you must assume that you need to keep in tune with what the future you may need, whether it be better discipline, knowledge or self-perception.

TO STEP INTO THE FUTURE YOU DESIRE, YOU MUST ACTIVELY SHIFT YOUR PERCEPTION OF YOURSELF TO BECOME WHO YOU NEED TO BE AS YOU CONTINUE TO GROW. THEN YOU CAN ACCEPT THE INFINITE POSSIBILITIES INTO YOUR CURRENT REALITY AS IT EXPANDS.

If you have grown up in an environment where you were told, **"YOU'RE NOT SMART ENOUGH,"** **"YOU'RE NOT CUTE ENOUGH,"** OR **"YOU'RE TOO LAZY, YOU NEVER FINISH ANYTHING,"** then your number one job is to replace those outdated beliefs. They are an impediment to your ability to become the person you dream of and to realize the sum of the equation — **OUTCOME**$^\infty$.

Your daily habits are another place to expand. The brain is a "**PLAY IT AGAIN, SAM**" kind of machine and loves routine. The amygdala, left to play on its own, will do everything it can to keep you safe, so you don't embarrass yourself. Playing safe, however, will not get you to the breakthroughs that you need to make to achieve outcomes greater than your current imaginings.

BY RAISING YOUR AWARENESS TO CONSCIOUSLY OBSERVE AND PARTICIPATE IN HOW YOUR BRAIN AUTOMATICALLY WORKS WITH, AND ON, THE CREATIVE GENIUS EQUATION, YOU'LL BUILD YOUR AGILITY VERSUS YOUR SUBCONSCIOUS AUTOMATON.

LET'S TAKE ONE MORE LOOK AT OUR EQUATION:

IMAGINATION: the ability to form new images and sensations in the mind that are not perceived through senses such as sight, hearing or other senses. This is you imagining the best possible outcome∞ for any situation and then shifting your perspective to see and integrate alternatives. **IMAGINATION IS A PORTAL TO THINGS YOU NEVER THOUGHT OF TRYING OR THOUGHT WERE POSSIBLE.**

INTUITION: your ability to understand something immediately without conscious reasoning. This is your inner sense of what will bring you a better outcome∞ and which of the action steps you imagine will be the best one to take right now. That subtle nudge is the link to the wormhole in the universe that can see you achieving a goal more quickly or eliminating a habit, step or process that is unnecessary. Ask yourself "**WHAT CAN I LET GO OF SO THAT THIS GOAL BECOMES THE PRIORITY?**" Watch out for your attachment to things you have already put in place, these can often slow down your ability to respond to any nudge in a new direction you may get.

DESIRE: that strong feeling of wanting something new to happen. This is your passion for a project, thing or experience, that will sustain you during the rough patches. When you complete an action, it will trigger your chemistry to believe you can reach your dream. Your success will continually fuel your passion, excitement and enthusiasm. **CONFIDENCE IS THE BIPRODUCT OF PRIOR PERFORMANCE** and the more challenging the task you achieve, the higher your confidence in handling more challenging tasks in the future.

DRIVE: to cause or guide your movement and carry you rigorously through to the finish line. Fueled by desire, it is the motivation, the internal condition, that aligns behavior and gives it direction. This is the muscle you build when you stay late, work smarter, keep working at your dream, and iterate the things you are doing to continue down the track. **THIS IS NOT TO BE CONFUSED WITH WORKING HARDER**. One of the ways to enhance your efficacy, is to have a clear goal of what it is you will accomplish in the time frame you set for yourself. Then, go back and fill your fuel tank of motivation. Close your eyes, remove any distractions (phone, noise, visual stimulation), take some deep breaths and imagine how you will feel when the task has already been accomplished. Sprinkle this daydream with thoughts like, "**WOW, THAT HAPPENED SO MUCH FASTER THAN I EVER IMAGINED IT WOULD!**" or "**IT'S AMAZING HOW THE RIGHT PEOPLE SHOWED UP AT THE RIGHT TIME TO OFFER HELP.**" Then open your eyes and do something towards your goal. Call someone, open your laptop and write, or draw out the roadmap for your next few months.

When you are passionate about what you are doing and you are fully engaged, you can tap into your own "flow" state where time appears to stop and you are fully immersed in the activity itself. This is the most amazing part of ourselves, that we can enter into an altered, flow state whenever we are working on anything with passion and focus. When we are in that flow state, we tap into a part of ourselves that operates all the time without our knowledge. It is the link between our physical and our spiritual selves. It is what I call your **CREATIVE GENIUS.**

BEST NEW START UP

OUTCOME

All equations end in a solution and an outcome. The outcome you discover from the **CREATIVE GENIUS EQUATION** is the ability to tap into a limitless pool of possibility. How your experience will turn out, the consequence, result or end-product is often better than you could ever have imagined.

It's the incredible part of change, how a sequence of moments in time and action towards a dream or goal works to help you grow. It's as if with each challenge, you are fine-tuning yourself to be able to step more fully into that new reality.

The **CREATIVE GENIUS EQUATION** is an innate and essential part of you. It's the magnetic equation that taps into the reticular activating system to reflect back the image and experiences of a life you desire. It's a tool to help you find a way through any obstacle you face so you can serve the universe, doing the work you have passion for, and which fulfills you.

> WHEN YOU DEDICATE TIME, FOCUS AND ENERGY TO CREATING THE LIFE YOU WANT, THE MORE YOU LOOK FOR WHAT'S MISSING AND THEN DECIDE WHICH LEVER TO PULL TO KEEP MOVING FORWARD.

If you start with asking, "**WHAT IS MY PURPOSE?**" you can apply the **CREATIVE GENIUS EQUATION** to reset your inner dial to the unique service in the world that only you can provide. If you are creating a vision for your life or your business, the **CREATIVE GENIUS EQUATION** can help you remember an inner dream that you had long forgotten.

Every year, I receive dozens of stories like this one from Jorge, who wrote,

"I WANTED TO DO VOICE-OVER WORK MY WHOLE LIFE AND WHEN I FIRST TRIED IT, I WASN'T THAT GOOD AT IT. MY MOTHER SUGGESTED I GO BACK TO SCHOOL TO LEARN TO TEACH ENGLISH AS A SECOND LANGUAGE BUT IT WASN'T MY PASSION. WHEN I DREW MY PICTURE OF MY DESIRED NEW REALITY AND MY FUTURE ME, THERE IT WAS! THERE IN THE PICTURE — ME DOING VOICE-OVER. I HAD TO GO BACK TO THE PART OF ME THAT I HAD DISCARDED WHEN IT GOT TOO SCARY. NOW I'M A SUCCESSFUL VOICE-OVER TALENT."

When you first embark on your dream and perhaps don't have success immediately, you may get caught by your brain's monitor, that part of you that is expecting a certain time frame. Rather than letting yourself get caught in the old patterns that accompanied any similar feelings of failure in the past, you can choose between giving up or positively reappraising what you are experiencing. Tell yourself this "failure" is an opportunity to learn more about where you need to shift and grow your skills. Your flexibility allows you to push through the obstacles and take your focused actions to the next level, where you will find success.

Jon Acuff writes in his book **DO OVER**,

> "CHANGING A DREAM ALWAYS REQUIRES LEARNING NEW SKILLS — EVEN IF THEY ARE SIMPLY NEW COPING SKILLS. I DIDN'T GET TO BE A PUBLIC SPEAKER BY NOT PUBLIC SPEAKING."

Most of us are not naturally brilliant at something the first time out of the gate, so trying something new helps you know if you will love doing it. But you cannot expect to know whether you will love this new venture unless you are willing to approach it with discipline and commitment.

When we watch online singing competitions like **THE VOICE**, the backstory is important. In that backstory you learn how performers practiced for countless hours to be able to step onto that stage. Being seen by millions is one opportunity but not every singer is able to get a chair to turn or move on in the competition. Those who realize that life doesn't happen to you, it happens for you, see every experience as valuable. While you practice and learn and hone your skills, each obstacle you encounter will help shape and fine tune you. It will give you clarity on what you truly love so you can let go of what you don't. Each experience will transform you as you step through the challenges to create the new you.

WHAT CAN LIFT YOU AND HELP YOU REFLECT ON WHAT YOU ARE LEARNING IS DEVELOPING A CONSISTENT MINDFULNESS PRACTICE.

When I first started meditating, at first nothing happened. I was distracted, my toe itched, I thought about the clients I was dealing with or the gardening that needed doing. But each day I sat back down in my chair to meditate again. I thought, "**OTHER PEOPLE ARE ABLE TO SIT STILL. WHY CAN'T I?**" Sometimes I would only last five minutes, other times I would look at the clock and be astonished that twenty minutes had passed. I yearned for inner guidance and an experience to know there was a way to gain a bigger perspective on what I was doing. It took two months of this discipline of sitting down, closing my eyes, imagining myself looking down on myself from up above, before I began to see results and had that powerful, ecstatic experience beyond anything that words could describe. To this day it's that deep experience and the consistent proof that I can tap into outcome∞ that brings me back to that chair, to that practice, to that inner space of exploration.

Your experience of growing your business or changing your health or experiencing love is uniquely yours. The beauty of life is that you get to discover and learn from your own inner and outer experiences. Those experiences keep fueling your enthusiasm and persistence, giving you greater awareness of how to do your work and how you find your path. By sitting down and getting quiet, we are simply listening for the next steps to take. That inner reflection inherently builds the knowledge that an outcome∞ and future-you is possible. In fact, it is your innate birthright.

As I work with young people just starting their careers, I hear about their anxiousness about the future. They wonder, "**DO I KNOW ENOUGH? AM I DISCIPLINED ENOUGH? AM I SMART ENOUGH?**"

All of us carry the seeds of these limiting beliefs. Each of us has the power to shift them. The biggest tip is to simply sit down and get still enough to hear the voice of **CREATIVE GENIUS YOU**. Once you are quiet, you can replay any positive experience in your mind. That image or daydream will help you sustain enthusiasm to get back to work, to remember you can do it. You are consistently programming your mind when you remember that fantastic presentation you gave or the comment from your boss about your work. Then you can ask a simple question about your next step and use your intuition to help you decide what to do next.

By working and evolving your thought patterns, you'll rewire your neural pathways towards success. And yep, at times it will be scary. A famous comic once called out an apology from a neighboring bathroom stall, before both of us were about to go onstage. "**YOU GOTTA PUSH OUT THE PEANUT BUTTER AND THEN COMES THE MIRACLE**." Today that comic plays key roles in many a popular Netflix series.

Once you recognize and claim responsibility for the creation of your world, you will build the courage to step up your game. You can then work to reframe any experience to continue to learn and grow. You'll know that it's you in that arena showing the doubters your biggest badass self; it's you that's willing to leap into the fire.

AT TIMES YOU'LL BE AN AMAZING, BEAUTIFUL FIREWORK, OTHER TIMES YOU MIGHT BE A DAMP SQUIB. BOTH THINGS WILL MOVE YOU TOWARDS THE LIFE YOU WANT.

QUICK RECAP BEFORE WE MOVE ON

1. **OUTCOMES∞ WILL ALWAYS EXCEED YOUR EXPECTATIONS** because your imagination is often limited by the brain's natural caution.

2. **OUTCOMES∞ TAKE TIME** so don't be discouraged if things take longer that you expect. Just because things didn't work out right away doesn't make you a failure.

3. **IF YOU DOUBT YOUR OWN ABILITY, GET QUIET** and let your Creative Genius have the space it needs to see the positive in you.

EXERCISE: ACTIVATION

TO CREATE OUTCOME∞ you need to apply the components of the equation. Ask yourself the following questions to help tap into each of the elements.

IMAGINATION:

- How well do I use this part of me?

- How could I draw it out — through journaling or visuals, through image or music?

INTUITION:

- How often do I listen to that subtle whisperer?

- What could I do today to harness its power better?

DESIRE:

- Which elements of what I am doing am I the most passionate about?

- Which projects need a refresh or positive reappraisal to reboot my enthusiasm?

DRIVE:

- Where do I need to work smarter?

- What flexible structure can I put in place to ensure I am focused on things that matter?

Map these elements out for yourself, so you can see how you are doing right now and identify just a few simple things you can tweak to see if you can feel greater alignment with your purpose and your destiny.

7. UNLOCKING CREATIVE GENIUS YOU

When you were at school, studying math, did you ever think (or even argue with your teacher), **"I GET HOW TO DO THIS BUT SO WHAT? WHAT'S THE POINT OF ALGEBRA OR CALCULUS OR GEOMETRY?"** Unless you are fascinated by math for math's sake, it's a pretty safe bet that you did.

So maybe now you are feeling the same about the **CREATIVE**

GENIUS EQUATION. I SEE HOW IMAGINATION PLUS INTUITION PLUS DESIRE PLUS DRIVE GIVE ME OUTCOME∞ BUT WHAT NOW? HOW DO I GET THIS TO WORK FOR ME? The reason I've shared the **CREATIVE GENIUS EQUATION** with you is because, whatever your idea, **IMAGINATION, INTUITION, DESIRE** and **DRIVE** are the four pivot points to get you to where you want to be.

In her book, **SOUL SOURCED ENTREPRENEUR**, Christine Kane speaks eloquently about evolution of an idea and suggests that the process is far more important than the outcome. In the book she defines a "New Ops Manual" which consists of eight "Guidelines for the Soul Track." Number four is: "**BECOMING IS THE NEW GETTING.**"

She writes of how we start at Point A (which I would call the "Current Reality") and the things we want are at Point B (in **DRAW YOUR FUTURE**® that is "Desired New Reality"). "**IN THE OLD SCHOOL MODEL,**" she writes, "**WE SPRINT AS FAST AS POSSIBLE, WITH ALL OUR DETERMINATION AND MIGHT TO SEIZE POINT B. WE ACHIEVE**

THINGS, WE GRAB THINGS, WE WRESTLE THINGS TO THE GROUND." This, Kane describes as the **"GIMME"** method, where we try to get things — people, clients, money, rich. And she adds, **"THE ENERGY OF GETTING IS SAD. IT'S ISOLATING. IT LEAVES YOU WIRED UP AND WIRY."**

Reading that chapter of her book woke me up. I realized I too had been caught in this thinking. In some of my promotional emails I was even suggesting you **"GO FROM GOAL SETTING TO GOAL GETTING!"** And yet, what I discovered from Kane's book was that the process is so much more potent than achieving the goal. What's more, the goal is far wider than just one singular thing.

IT ALL COMES DOWN TO WHY WE ARE REALLY HERE. My perspective is that we are here to learn to love — to love better and deeper and accept ourselves and other people. We are learning to share and expand; to give service to all of life.

That doesn't mean you are going to give it away all the time, or not learn the necessary steps to run your business or write that book. It just means you realize you are part of a bigger picture and the essential part you play in it. The goal, then, is self-awareness and expansion and, along the way, maybe we will make money or collaborate with new people or find a new soulmate or enjoy new hobbies or visit new places.

IN THE PROCESS, YOU WILL LEARN TO LISTEN BETTER TO THE VOICE THAT CALLS YOU TOWARDS YOUR INNER DREAM.

You'll learn better how to hire the right talent at the right time. You'll come to understand that you have a gift and it will be unique and beautiful. And if a business or career is what you seek, you can grow to package it and offer it to customers in a meaningful way that aligns with you. You have access to everything you need to know and the means to find the things you don't know so you can hire people to help you fulfill your purpose and turn your dreams into reality.

Following are a few simple ways to adjust what you are doing to align yourself to this concept of growth and maturity.

TOOLS FOR IMAGINATION

WHITEBOARD YOUR QUESTION

VISUAL THINKING is one of the easiest ways to get an answer to any question you have. You simply need to give yourself the space (literally, with a clean whiteboard) to explore your question. It might be **"SHOULD I STAY IN THIS CAREER?" "IS THIS FOOD GOOD FOR ME?" "HOW CAN I BE MORE FINANCIALLY SOUND?"** Visual problem solving can amplify what you need to hear.

With piece of paper and pen in hand, or with a whiteboard nearby, imagine you are walking into a classroom. Then on that whiteboard or paper write out your question. Sit for a few minutes with your eyes closed, asking your question a couple of times in your mind. Take a deep breath and tune it.

As soon as you get any kind of a nudge or subtle answer to your question, write or draw whatever comes to you. If you don't understand what you have written down, or don't "get" anything, write that down and continue to write until an idea comes through. Look for small actions you can take to create a shift in the situation you are asking about. While the answer might be "be patient," if you need something more specific, ask for it.

When I envision my imagination, I see it as a team; an army of assistants who work to create new neural pathways between ideas and concepts to help me problem solve. I imagine that they are just hanging out there, quietly sifting through the waters of my memories in my hippocampus, silently waiting — like a stage crew in the alley on a smoke break — until I give them something to do.

When you snap your fingers and point to your desired outcome∞ they are at the ready, all action, mocking up the set design and costumes to help you step on stage into that future — lights, camera, action! But without direction that smoke break can go on for hours or days or years. Without positive direction, they will sift through your past, dredging up old patterns and tossing a limiting belief onto the turntable of your thoughts. Sometimes they can't figure out what to do with your anxiety or worry, so they find a secret spot in your body to hide it. You get to wrangle your team. Why not give them a job to do? Set them going with a specific task: "**I NEED TO MEET SOMEONE WHO CAN HELP ME FURTHER MY CAREER.**" "**I AM LOOKING FOR A LIFE PARTNER WHO IS KIND, LOVING, A GOOD COMMUNICATOR AND LOVES MY CHILDREN.**"

They'll go to work lining up that experience. You can make sure it is coming to you by feeding them positive images to expand upon and build that ongoing mural in your mind. Heighten your senses so you'll be prepared to see, know, be and do. And ask that amazing imagination team, **WHAT IS ONE THING YOU WOULD RECOMMEND THAT I DO RIGHT NOW TOWARDS THAT GOAL?** Then, whatever answer you get, don't delay, go do it!

Galvanize that imagination crew to get busy on those outcomes∞ by rewarding them with gratitude. Mockup a desired change you want in one area of your life. Gain clarity about it using one of the visual tips shared in this book, and take action to step into that new you, knowing that your Creative Genius is with you. Then, give thanks for anything that comes your way.

100 QUESTIONS

This exercise comes from my great friend, Pete Cohen's book, **INSPIRATORS**.

Find some time where you will not be disturbed and write down 100 questions to ask yourself. They can be questions about absolutely anything: **WHY IS THE SKY BLUE? WHAT IS THE MEANING OF LIFE? WHY AM I READING THIS BOOK? HOW DO I FIX THE BROKEN TABLE LEG?**

When you go through this process, the first few will just probably flow and then you'll get to a point where you feel that you can't think of any more. Keep going. You'll start to tune in to the questions you are asking yourself:

HOW DO I IMPROVE MY HEALTH?

HOW DO I BECOME A BETTER LEADER?

WHAT IF I HAD MY OWN TIME MACHINE?

HOW DO I BECOME A BETTER PARTNER TO MY SPOUSE?

WHAT WAS THE NAME OF THAT COOL APP FRAN SHOWED ME LAST NIGHT?

WHAT DOES A TRULY GREAT DAY LOOK LIKE FOR ME?

WHEN DO I FEEL MOST ALIVE?

HOW CAN I TAKE BETTER CARE OF MYSELF?

WHY DOES A GIRAFFE HAVE A LONG NECK?

HOW CAN I MANAGE MY EMOTIONS MORE EFFECTIVELY?

Once you have at least 100 questions, start looking for themes. Do not judge the questions — just group them around business, health, family, self-growth, money, general curiosity, fantastical ideas and so on.

Then, take the 10 questions that are most significant to you and within that top 10, rank them in order of importance. The one that you rank as most important is your Key Question.

Now write it down on a card or piece of paper, where you can see it every day. Contemplate that question. Ask it of yourself every day, maybe several times a day, for a few days or a few weeks. Then maybe when you feel you have an answer that takes you forward, pick another question or repeat the whole exercise.

THIS IS AN EXERCISE THAT I DID YEARS AGO AND IT FUNDAMENTALLY CHANGED MY LIFE. THE NUMBER ONE QUESTION MANY YEARS AGO WAS, "HOW DO I GET PAID TO DO WHAT I LOVE DOING?" I THOUGHT ABOUT THAT QUESTION A LOT.

CREATIVE GENIUS BEHAVIOR CHANGE

Using your imagination to move yourself forward is very powerful, but you can also use it just as effectively to help change a behavior that you want to enhance or doesn't serve you any longer.

Choose a behavior you'd like to change, like your habit of interrupting others when you get excited or leaving the top off the toothpaste. You get the idea…

1. Think of the behavior you would like to change.

2. Find a quiet place where you can be alone and uninterrupted for at least 30 minutes. Close your eyes, take a few deep breaths and breathe this way until you feel calm. You want to become calm enough to shift yourself into an alpha state of consciousness.

3. Shift your awareness to your body, the beating of your heart, the sound of your breath as it moves in and out. Tune your awareness to your lungs as they expand and contract,

then notice the space around them. As you increase your awareness of the space around your body and the space within your body, you'll increase your alignment with the energy field that already exists around you. As you deepen your awareness of the rhythm of your heart and your breath, the space within you and around you, you will automatically move into a deeper state of calm.

3. Now visualize the behavior you want to let go of. This might feel at first difficult to imagine, as we usually don't like these things about ourselves, but let it clearly emerge in your mind's eye. Once you have it, take the image you have before you and imagine that you are putting it into a big box. Notice that there is an elevator in front of you, with the doors wide open. Get into the elevator with your box and ride to the highest floor. When the doors open, imagine a balcony in front of you. Walk over to the edge of the balcony and hold your box out over the edge. Feel and hear a strong wind coming towards you, it is so strong that you have no choice but to release the box and let it be blown out and into the sky by the wind. As the wind carries

the box away, the behavior you put inside falls out and is carried away. Watch as your unwanted behavior breaks into tiny pieces and is scattered by the wind in every direction.

4. Now think of a behavior you would like to enhance in yourself. Image how you would look and feel if you were behaving in this positive way. Visualize yourself being filled with the new behavior as if were warm sunlight pouring into you. Imagine it fully and give thanks for the possibility of this new dimension of yourself. Savor this feeling for as long as you like.

5. Now visualize yourself going back into the elevator. As you ride down, imagine that you are being drawn to this new behavior as if by a powerful magnet. Imagine even more deeply what it feels like to fully integrate this new trait, this new way of being. See yourself in your mind's eye behaving this new way in future interactions people, places, things as you move through your daily life.

6. End the meditation by opening your eyes, stretching a bit and getting grounded. Then go about your day and pay

particular attention to small shifts in how you react to different situations you encounter. Expect to be surprised. If you notice the behavior you discarded getting triggered, as quickly as possible catch yourself and replace the old behavior with your new one. Then stop and be grateful. Gratitude is the emotion that helps lock the new way of being into place. Try to do this meditation practice using the imagination described above as often as you can, until you have integrated this new behavior fully.

TOOLS FOR INTUITION

YOUR INTERNAL FOCUS GROUP

This process is useful when you are wondering about the next step to take — maybe new content for your course, or a new exercise routine to follow or how to handle a difficult personality.

Start by sitting at your desk with your laptop open. Then using your imagination, mockup an internal focus group. Their job is to fill in the gaps about what you've read online or heard in interviews about your subject matter, for instance clients, group dynamics or effective methods for fitness. Then, keyboard in front of you, open a new document and ask your imaginary focus group to give you a few bullet points of ideas you should consider. Type them out and ask for further clarification. What you are tapping into, by using any open document, is your Creative Genius. When you assume more answers will come when needed, they will.

When you go to pick up a glass of water, your brain, which is dealing with a two-dimensional optic eye, will fill in the gap between what the eye sees and where that glass is. Let your Creative Genius fill the gaps to provide you with the raw materials you need to ensure your presentation, meeting, fitness plan hits the mark. This process of gathering data from your internal focus group is the first step in the process, the next is to use your intuition to choose from the ideas and decide which one will serve you the best. I trust my inner knowing, but I "tie up my camel" by comparing this to any criteria I have already created for success — using either a cost/benefit analysis or another simple sorting process.

PENDULUM-YOU

Sometimes you can gain insight and simple "yes/no" answers by using yourself as a pendulum.

You read that sentence correctly. Your body can be used as a pendulum to test what is good for you. Here's a simple way to do it. First, stand and close your eyes and say the words "**YES, YES, YES.**" Then see how your body responds. Once you know what "**YES**" feels like, then say the words, "**NO, NO, NO.**" Get clear on what no feels like in your body. Often it will lean forward for yes and backwards for no. I test it again by saying, "**MY NAME IS JOHN,**" and wait for the pull backwards. And then "**MY NAME IS PATTI**" which should lean my body forwards.

YES

YES

YES

Now let's put it to the test on something simple like food. If you want to know if a food is good for you, hold that food in your hand, or the product you are about to buy, and press it against your stomach. Now, close your eyes and ask, "**IS THIS SOMETHING THAT WILL BE GOOD FOR ME?**"

Stand still and feel which way your body wants to lean. See which way your body leans with this food or product. The way it moves will guide you to "**YES**" or "**NO**." If you have never done this before, test it a couple of times until you feel certain of the answer. Try this kind of yes/no testing for yourself. It will turn up the volume on your subconscious.

GET QUIET — TURN YOUR EGO DOWN

How do you turn up the volume on your Creative Genius and turn down your ego? The ego's job is to boost your self-esteem, so let's be clear: you need it to survive in this world. You just don't want your ego to be in the driver's seat all the time. I can tell that ego is driving when I find myself trying to make me right and others wrong. Ego wants to make you to feel like you are better than everyone else in the world. "**THAT GUY'S GREAT, BUT YOU'RE THE BEST!**"

The Creative Genius is the quieter part of you that speaks to you in the moments when you're in a calm (alpha) state. Accessing that alpha state can easily be done with some of the techniques I have mentioned before like square breathing meditation. Or it can be while running, cycling, swimming; any activity where your body is concentrating on maintaining pace. You can bring it on by a shower or by writing or drawing a picture.

THE CREATIVE GENIUS LIVES IN THE 'FLOW STATE'. THERE ARE NO LIMITS IN FLOW. YOU ARE BEYOND THE SUBCONSCIOUS MIND AND IN A STATE OF ALTERED AWARENESS BROUGHT ON BY THE FOCUS AND INTENSITY OF YOUR ATTENTION.

Recently I caught a horrendous cold and it was so bad I had to actually stay in bed for ten days while I recovered. When I wasn't sleeping, I read fiction, daydreamed and relaxed. My type-A personality wanted me to jump up and work but every time I tried, I was overcome with pure exhaustion. One afternoon, I felt a little better. My brain urged me to get up, warning me, "**WOW, YOU ARE WAY BEHIND! YOU BETTER GET SOME WORK DONE!**" In the three-hour time span that followed, I got more done on major projects than I had in the weeks building up to being sick. I wrote a couple of talks I had been putting off, drew the visuals to go with them, and mapped my own future for the next year. Then, just for fun, I rearranged my office to make it more relaxing and reading materials more accessible. When I looked at the clock, I couldn't believe how many things I had gotten done in such a short period of time.

What had happened? It was as if all that time lying in bed, I had been simmering on ideas. Since I didn't have my normal defenses up, my Creative Genius had free rein with my imagination. My openness allowed the new ideas to pour in.

WRITING
OR DRAWING
ALLOWS THE CHILDLIKE
PART OF YOU
TO CHANNEL
WHATEVER VOICES
AND VISION
TO COME THROUGH
TO THE PAGE.

ANNE LAMOTT

WAKE UP YOUR RAS

I mentioned the power of your Reticular Activating System earlier and the power it has to notice and attract answers. Here is a way to give it a tune up and see more of the right messages.

1. Find a quiet place where you won't be disturbed. Sit comfortably, close your eyes, and begin to take some deep breaths to shift yourself into a relaxed state. Focus on your breath or try some four-part breathing (we mentioned that way back in Chapter 1). From this relaxed state, call to mind a situation or event around which you want more clarity. In this alpha state, inwardly ask for some insight about it, both in the moment and in the days to come. Then, open your eyes and go about your day while paying attention to anything that stands out as something unusual that has happened to or around you.

2. Pull your intuition into the present moment by getting a piece of paper and relaxing using any breathing technique that works for you. Then ask, "**WHAT DO I NEED RIGHT NOW**

IN MY LIFE?" Allow the ideas to flow through you onto the paper in words or images. As soon as you hear or sense something inwardly, capture it. If you find yourself distracted, simply close your eyes, and repeat the process to ask again.

3. Focus on a particular sense for 24 hours to heighten your awareness of it. You might choose touch, sight, hearing, taste, or gut reactions. Ask, "**HOW CAN USING MY INTUITION THROUGH THIS SENSE HELP TO INFORM ME IN DECISION MAKING?**" Write down anything you learn.

4. Intuition can come through any type of "**WAKING DREAM**" symbols. It may be billboards, songs on the radio or Internet or license plates for example. Ask for a sign through a literal sign and see what your next step is. Write down anything you experience or see.

5. Interact with nature and assign signs to help you; a flower might mean opportunity, a stone could represent a challenge. Treat the world around you as if you are in a constant dialogue with it. Assume everything is happening on

your behalf and see how it broadens your perspective of what's possible.

TOOLS FOR DESIRE

TUNE YOUR CREATIVE GENIUS TO THE ENERGY FIELD THAT SURROUNDS YOU

We live in a time when people and the planet need your attention and love. Yes, you can improve your life and bring more of your Creative Genius forward for your own growth but what if you could expand the field of love that is you to spread out and touch others, without getting in their space or trying to change them? Maybe you are involved in a work situation that holds some conflict or unexpressed emotions. Perhaps you have a relationship with someone that needs some finetuning to be more equal or open. Or it could be your own unhealthy habits aren't setting the best example to those around you.

Attuning yourself to the energy field swirling in and around you helps expand your level of awareness and capacity to love. One of the easiest ways to attune yourself is through chanting or singing. You might start by singing a tone, maybe a vowel or an uplifting phrase. Spell a word out in song, like L-O-V-E, sing each letter as a long drawn out tone. Sing it to the universe either quietly inside or out loud. Sing it when you feel fear or want to know truth about what you might be facing. Sing the word Allelujah, Allah, AUM or HU. Or create your own mantra. I like, "**I BRING LOVE INTO EVERY MOMENT.**" Singing an uplifting inner song when people are fighting in your presence, will bring calm to the environment.

CHANTING OR SINGING HELPS YOU TO MERGE WITH A TANGIBLE, PHYSICAL FORCE FIELD BEHIND EVERYTHING AND EVERYBODY. CHANTING A WORD THAT UPLIFTS YOU WILL HELP YOU FIND PEACE WHEN YOU FEEL TROUBLED AND BALANCE WHEN YOU FEEL STRESSED.

You can also listen to the sounds all around you: the birds in the morning, the reverberating, high pitched sound you hear when the fridge clicks on and off, even the din of the traffic. It turns up the volume on the you that's behind all the chatter and the petty stuff that you might find yourself caught up in. Bring your true self forward, and find your own word, sound, tone, song or mantra that helps you open your heart.

When you raise your awareness to how your energy impacts others and take responsibility for it, you realize you are no longer subject to your emotions. Then you can control them to bring more positivity to your environment.

DECIDE TO BE INSPIRED

> SINCE INTENTION IS POWERFUL, YOUR CHOICE TO BE INSPIRED WILL DETERMINE EVERYTHING.

Before you get out of bed, decide that you will be inspired that day, then look for the inspiration. Be grateful in advance for what is coming your way. Close your eyes and imagine yourself in the life you have been dreaming. Start the day with a visceral sense of what it feels like to succeed. Immerse yourself, even momentarily, in that feeling. What will others be saying about you? What will you be saying about yourself? Imagine that feeling of success filling you from the bottoms of your feet to the top of your head and let yourself be deeply grateful for what is to come.

FIND WHAT INSPIRES YOU

Cultivate sources of inspiration so you are surrounded by positive energy. Find books, podcasts and videos that spark your inspiration. Make reviewing or listening to them part of what you do on a regular basis to stay on track. As you listen or read, make some notes about what catches your attention until you feel inspired to jump back into your own project.

This isn't a once-and-done exercise either. Keep looking out for things which inspire you and keep adding to your collection.

CHOP WOOD CARRY WATER

Oddly enough, we often find that some of our best ideas come to us when we're doing something completely mundane and not even remotely related to our goals. When you take a break from focused attention and do some mindless task, your brain has a chance to reboot itself. Next time you feel stuck or overwhelmed, try taking a 30-minute nap, clean out the junk drawer, or pull weeds for a while to see what emerges.

TOOLS FOR DRIVE

PLAYING THE "YES... AND" GAME

This is a great way to trick yourself out of routine behaviors and patterns of resistance. You probably remember this from any improvisation class or business negotiation training you took, either by choice or because you were forced into it! The participants (actors) in the "YES... AND" game must incorporate whatever is given to them as a line or object in an improvisational scene by saying, "YES... AND" and continuing to expand and incorporate that new idea into the narrative.

In a recent client engagement, I found myself getting more and more upset as the clients picked apart my images. I jumped through hoop after hoop, attempting to please them. I watched as hour upon unpaid hour ticked by. It wasn't just the time I was putting in; it was the headspace that it took up. I would wake in the middle of the night and lie there thinking about how mad I was about the situation.

Then one day I realized that by putting so much attention on the challenge, I was making the situation worse. I'd been so resistant to the client that my resistance had become the problem. I decided to secretly play the **"YES... AND"** game with them (and myself). I accepted that they needed to make these changes and decided that no matter what they gave me, I would just say **"YES"** and keep moving. The shift was dramatic, mostly because it allowed me to let go.

The client said the illustration was too vibrant. (**"YES... AND"**) I said, **"I CAN FIX THAT."**

"THIS OBJECT NEEDS TO BE MOVED FURTHER TO THE LEFT," they said.

"(YES... AND) EASY PEASY," I said. It took all of five minutes in Photo-shop to shift it over.

"YES AND, DO YOU LIKE IT BETTER HERE?" I asked.

They did! Suddenly the project moved forward with ease.

"OH YAH, YAH," you scoff, on the other end of this one-way dialogue. **"RESOLUTION TO ISSUES ISN'T ALWAYS THAT EASY!"**

YES... AND DON'T TAKE MY WORD FOR IT, TRY IT YOURSELF.

THE MAGIC ERASER

Upping your Creative Genius is about being willing to approach what's vexing you with an attitude of play and fun. Clearly there's a whole population of people out there dedicated to taking themselves super-seriously. Why follow that flock? Flex your creative muscles by challenging your crabbiness and leaping over it, using any technique possible.

My wife Julie used to be completely bugged by my (sometimes) inability to listen before trying to fix something she was working through. She'd be telling me something and I'd be trying to solve it before she even got the whole story out. This would push her buttons and steam would start coming out of her ears.

I learned that if I was paying attention, I could quickly interrupt the pattern by using a drama therapy technique I learned in my training. I'd say, **"HEY THAT DIDN'T GO SO WELL, CAN I USE THE MAGIC ERASER AND TRY IT AGAIN?"** I'd pretend to erase the air in front of us, then sit down again and start the conversation over. Better results! Try it with your clients, partner or child.

VUJA DE — TURN YOUR WORLD UPSIDE DOWN (FOR BETTER IDEAS)

Sometimes you need to look at things from different angles to gain a new perspective. Adam Grant writes in his book **ORIGINALS,**

"VUJA DE IS THE REVERSE — WE FACE SOMETHING FAMILIAR, BUT WE SEE IT WITH A FRESH PERSPECTIVE. THAT ENABLES US TO GAIN NEW INSIGHTS INTO OLD PROBLEMS. THE HALLMARK OF ORIGINALITY IS REJECTING THE DEFAULT AND EXPLORING WHETHER A BETTER OPTION EXISTS."

To see how this can work, let me tell you of a time when I had a real live (not imaginary), Creative Genius team.

I'd been invited to create a mural for the Seattle Space Needle that would inspire the employees as they walked down the hallway of the employee entrance. While I am a strategic illustrator and have drawn huge, 12–15-foot drawings, I am not a muralist. In fact, I draw in pen and pastels on paper and I have absolutely no mural nor painting experience, so I knew I was going to need help.

I called up one of my favorite collaborators, Scott Ward, who has done a half dozen murals in the Pacific Northwest. "HEY SCOOTER, WANT TO PAINT A MURAL AT THE SPACE NEEDLE?"

Yes, he was up for the challenge! Together we interviewed employees for their stories, then I drew some preliminary sketches, Scott gave his Creative Genius input, cleaned up the drawings and the Space Needle approved the 34' x 4' mural.

We both fully anticipated being able to use markers on the wall, which was my typical medium. I'd done a small test using markers on a similarly painted wall in my garage at home, which seemed to go well. Subsequently, we went out and bought $800 of markers in all colors and went in, ready to "**KNOCK THIS MUTHA OUT**."

Using a projector, we projected the drawing onto the wall and pencil sketched the image late into the night. The next day, when we put the first marker to the wall, we were met with a big surprise. The pen pulled the paint right off the wall and immediately got all gummed up making it unusable. **OMG! THIS WASN'T GOING TO WORK!** It would take thousands of hours and three times the amount of markers to create the mural this way.

Clearly another solution was required. What now?

Quickly I had to turn up the volume on my Creative Genius, while trying not to poop my pants with the sheer terror of what I was facing.

"**YOU'LL HAVE TO PAINT IT**," my Creative Genius whispered. Paint it! What?! I'm not a painter! This would require skills I did not possess.

Guess what though?! I had hired one of the best painters in the city, my Creative Genius teammate, Scott Ward. We looked at each other and laughed, then got in the car, drove to the art supply store, returned the pens, and bought paint and paint markers instead.

Back at the Needle, Scott gave me a crash course in how to paint a mural. The new paint pens were almost like using markers, which made it easy to transfer my drawing skills to the wall and Scott finessed the parts of the mural that needed painting in his unique, whimsical style.

Wow, that was one of those experiences where I found myself literally up against a wall, begging my Creative Genius (and the universe) to help me figure it out. It required a ton of drive to get to completion, but pure awesomeness ensued. And it was the **CREATIVE GENIUS EQUATION** in reverse:

OUTCOME∞: What does your compelling vision look like? What does it feel like? AN AMAZING COOL MURAL IN THE EMPLOYEE ENTRANCE OF THE SPACE NEEDLE.

DRIVE: When is your deadline to make that change in yourself, your business or your world? WE HAD EXACTLY 3 DAYS TO FINISH THE MURAL!

DESIRE: Why do you really, really, really want this? THIS IS GOING TO INSPIRE THOUSANDS OF PEOPLE WHO WORK AT THE SPACE NEEDLE, SO THEY WILL GIVE AN EVEN BETTER EXPERIENCE FOR CUSTOMERS.

INTUITION: What process will access your gut and brain to filter your ideas to know which ones you can take action on? MARKERS WON'T WORK, SO WE NEED TO USE PAINT TO AVOID PULLING THE PAINT OFF THE WALL.

IMAGINATION: How can you use your imagination to help you come up with ideas? GET SCOTT'S HELP. TRY PAINT PENS.

This backwards approach is simple and shakes up your thinking so you can access different ideas, goals or processes. It's also a reminder that the **CREATIVE GENIUS EQUATION** is an interactive process and allows you to access different parts of the equation at different times, based on what you are solving.

During the 2020/21 pandemic we had to shift how we have done almost everything. We ordered food online or perhaps we delivered it. Our in-person meetings became virtual. We could have stayed at home helping our environment by cutting down on driving years ago, but we didn't. Suddenly we were forced to, and it turns out for some people it was better for their family.

GUESS WHAT? YOU GOT TO UP YOUR CREATIVE GENIUS" SKILLS. THAT WAS AND STILL IS AWESOME.

Look around, the world is chaotic right now, but it always has been for some people. Lots of people are struggling. The planet and its people need our talents to sustain the freedom we have earned and the beauty that surrounds us.

A transformative experience starts with one person: **YOU**.

> IF YOU WANT THINGS TO STAY STATIC THE RULE IS: KEEP DOING WHAT YOU'VE ALWAYS DONE. THE CATCH IS YOU CAN'T COMPLAIN ABOUT IT. YOU CAN'T JUST SAY YOU WANT THINGS TO BE DIFFERENT WITHOUT ACTIVATING YOUR CREATIVE GENIUS TO SERVE THE WORLD.

Now it's time for you to apply that vuja de to your life right now!

SEEING IT ALL IN ACTION

FEAR IS WONDERFUL

Fear is wonderful because it sparks your imagination. It opens you up to listen to your intuition. It forces you to see what you really desire and drive yourself out of disaster.

You probably know that I am a performance artist. For those who don't know what that is, it's a bit like being an actor except that you create your own material; usually some bad mime, a song you made up and some questionable dance routines. And then you subject an audience to it for an indeterminate amount of time. I started out doing street performances, passing a hat around and making some money that way. Then a friend of mine suggested that I go to New York and take some formal acting training. So I did.

One weekend I had a friend visiting from Seattle. While he was there, we went out for pizza and we passed through the Broadway district. My friend turned to me and said, "**HEY PATTI, DID YOU EVER WANT TO BE ON BROADWAY?**" "**FRANK,**" I said, "**I AM A PERFORMANCE ARTIST; I WOULD ONLY BE OFF-BROADWAY!**" But that idea stuck and I couldn't get it out if my head.

IMAGINATION — WHAT IF...

"WHAT IF I WAS ON BROADWAY?"

I'd go in through the stage door, into my dressing room where there'd be a star and my name on the door, and my costume laid out ready for me. I'd put on my make-up and go and stand behind that thick red velvet curtain waiting for them to call places and the lights to come down and that audience hush.

And it was thrilling. It was a great fantasy to have when I went back to Seattle where I was working at Mama's Mexican Kitchen just to scratch a crust. I'd think, "WELL, IF I WERE ON BROADWAY WHERE WOULD THE OPENING NIGHT PARTY BE? TAVERN ON THE GREEN! YES. AND IF I WERE ON BROADWAY, WELL WHO WOULD I BE HANGING OUT WITH? OH, LILY TOMLIN AND EDDIE MURPHY," (this was a while back) "COOL!" And then I put it out of my mind.

269

INTUITION — CHOPPING WOOD AND CARRYING WATER

Later that year, things got tough. I lost all my shifts at Mama's and the NEA stopped funding performance art so I didn't have enough money for my rent. I thought, "**WHAT AM I GOING TO DO?**" so I grabbed a rake, went to the wealthiest neighborhood in Seattle and started knocking door-to-door asking if I could rake people's yards for $10 a yard. I was a performance artist so my hair was chartreuse and I knocked and knocked and knocked and nobody opened their door (would you?). Eventually though, one door was opened by a minister whose yard was the size of a football field.

"SURE, YOU CAN RAKE MY YARD FOR $10."

It was a typical Seattle day, which means it was pouring with rain and the wind was howling. And I was out in this, raking and raking and the leaves were falling and I was raking and raking, over and over again.

Finally, the minister came out and shoved $10 at me and said, "**GO HOME!**" So I did. It was a real low point, but everything was telling me to keep going.

DESIRE — FEEL THE FEAR AND DO IT ANYWAY

When I got home, my answering machine was blinking. The first message was from my friend Karen. "**HEY PD, THEY'RE AUDITIONING PERFORMANCE ARTISTS DOWN THE SEATTLE REPERTORY THEATRE. YOU'VE GOT TO GO.**" And the next one was from my long-lost agent. "**PATTI, I THINK I'VE FINALLY FOUND AN OPPORTUNITY TO SHOWCASE YOUR UNIQUE TALENTS!**" So I called back immediately and got an audition.

The next day I went down to the theatre with my résumé and saw the line. It was snaking all the way around the block. But this is what I wanted. So I waited my turn.

When I finally get up to the front, they ask me to do a dance routine. I'm not a dancer! But I decide to give it my best shot anyway. They showed me a routine and I did the best I could, added some weird thing on the end and then fell down dead on the stage. And it was just quirky enough that I got into the show. And then this amazing thing happened. The show went from that small theater to the main stage at the Seattle Rep. And then six months later, it went from the Seattle Rep to the Kennedy Center in DC. And then six months later it went to…

BROADWAY!

Opening night party was at Tavern on the Green!

And during the run of the show who did I meet, Lily Tomlin and Eddie Murphy? Nope! Steve Martin and Robin Williams!

THE CREATIVE GENIUS EQUATION CHANGES EVERYTHING!

DRIVE — KEEPING GOING

I knew there was something about the inner picture I had created so I began to hack myself. "**HOW DID THAT HAPPEN? WHAT CAN I**

DO?" I began to imagine, **"WHAT IF I MADE THIS AMOUNT OF MONEY OR HAD THIS AMOUNT OF ACTING JOBS? WHAT WOULD HAPPEN?"**

I began to test and try and I must, at some point, have created a picture in my mind that I wasn't going to perform anymore because I went to Portland, Oregon and I put on a show on my own. After the first night I went to the news stand, got the papers and opened the review. And it said **"PATTI DOBROWOLSKI. CAN'T SING; CAN'T ACT; CAN'T DANCE; CAN'T WRITE; DON'T BOTHER."**

Wow, I was on Broadway and now this! What brought this change about?

There I was, weeping in the garden, my ego abandoning me because everything I knew about myself was that I was an actor and now I didn't know what to do. But that was the setback which took me to the life I have now. A friend suggested I retrain as a drama therapist (which I was terrible at. I kept telling people what to do: **"YOUR HUSBAND IS TERRIBLE, LEAVE HIM!" "YOU HAVE A DRINKING PROBLEM, GO TO AA"**) and that led me to become a consultant working with organizations and individuals, showing them how to draw their future.

EVERYTHING, IN FACT, THAT LED ME TO HERE.

BRING YOUR CREATIVE GENIUS TO LIFE

We all know that no two atoms are completely alike just as no one person's path is the same as another. Your journey through life will be unique to you, your choices are yours and yours alone.

Throughout this book I have been sharing tips from my own experience to help you find your own way, your own path. You have been curious enough to keep reading and open to learning how to connect to the greater good.

IF THERE IS ONE KEY THAT HELPED ME UNLOCK MY CAPACITY TO CHANGE MORE QUICKLY, IT WAS THIS: WHAT MATTERS IS WHAT I BELIEVE MATTERS.

Just like your own inner and outer picture of your dream of the future, only you see the fullness and depth of that dream. You are the connector to the Creative Genius in your own life. And when you come from this perspective, you'll find whatever you need to help you grow and realize your dream.

Whether you do or you don't envision a future, one will happen.

THE QUESTION IS, DO YOU WANT TO PARTICIPATE IN THE CREATION OR EXPLORATION OF THAT FUTURE? OR DO YOU WANT TO JUST LET THAT FUTURE UNFOLD FOR YOU?

Imagine you are just in a boat floating in the ocean. The ocean has its own cadence and rhythm. You can sit there as the sun rises and sets and allow the waves and current to move you this way or that. Or you can choose a direction to pursue and grab the oars and row.

If you randomly row without a sense of direction, you'll get tired, hungry and thirsty. And maybe that's the only experience that you want to have right now. But when you add a direction or goal or vision to your rowing, you begin the delicate interplay between you and the rest of the world.

The dialogue between you and nature, between you and the mysterious flow of life; this powerful dialogue will fill your life with meaning and purpose. This is the **CREATIVE GENIUS YOU** in action.

Suddenly you are no longer rowing in isolation, something begins to row with you and for you. The path between you and your destination becomes filled with wonder. And in that wonder is the magic and in that magic is **CREATIVE GENIUS YOU**. Envision your future, let your Creative Genius be your GPS and guide, grab your oars and let's go.

Big love,

PATTI

APPENDIX

APPLY THE CREATIVE GENIUS EQUATION TO YOUR SUCCESS

To help you work the **CREATIVE GENIUS EQUATION** in your own life, here is a checklist of questions and actions to step you through each part of it. It doesn't matter whether this is for a personal dream, a career aspiration or something affecting your life in a more wholistic way.

Use the questions to guide you and allow your Creative Genius to get going and flourish.

IMAGINATION: For the dream you have for your future — can you imagine it?

- Describe what it looks like when you have achieved success?

- And how will you feel when you are there?

- What will people around you be saying?

- What will you be saying?

DRAW A SIMPLE PICTURE OF WHAT SUCCESS LOOKS LIKE IN THIS EXPERIENCE.

INTUITION: With a close connection to where you want to go, let your intuition guide you on what you need to do next to move this process along, to step closer to that state of success? Brainstorm a few ideas here:

Now close your eyes and ask yourself — the part of you that truly knows all the facts and all the truth that is innate in your essence — what might I be missing? Write down anything that comes to you.

Finally, look at all your ideas for next steps and allow yourself to get quiet and ask, "**WHAT SHOULD I DO NEXT?**"

The choice should not be one out of guilt or obligation. It will feel exciting and perhaps somewhat scary.

DESIRE: Ask yourself **"WHAT IS IT THAT I REALLY, REALLY, REALLY WANT?"** Daydream about the world when you can have whatever you chose and where you can have it all.

Is this in alignment with who you are and what you are doing in the present moment?

When you cast your net into the future what exciting things are you doing and being?

What obstacles are you facing? Real or imagined?

Take steps to reset your focus to align it to what you truly desire.

DRIVE: To achieve what you truly desire, write a list of all the possible actions you could take to get you there. Don't worry if some of them scare you, or feel too hard, or are just plain wacky. List them all.

Now get quiet and ask:

- What small, immediate actions do you need to take?

- Is there anything you are avoiding doing? Why?

For each big action, break it down into small action steps that are easier to take. Find 1-2 things you can do right away.

GO AND DO SOMETHING TOWARDS YOUR GOAL, RIGHT NOW!

NOTES:

USING THE CREATIVE GENIUS EQUATION WITH A TEAM

The **CREATIVE GENIUS EQUATION** also applies to group efforts. So, whether you are in a corporate setting, a community group or even in a family, you can solve problems and create amazing outcomes by working together. Here's how:

SETTING THE SCENE

You came together for a reason, so start by identifying what your challenge/desired outcome(s) might be. For example:

- We're a new team, we need to get to know one another better.

- Our church council seems to be experiencing a lot of friction, we want to create alignment so we are doing good in the community.

- Or even, we want a family holiday we can all enjoy (without arguments)!

You might want to create a collective vision, address dissonance, set guiding principles for how you work together or build relationships. Any and all of these can be addressed in this way.

IMAGINATION: To tap into imagination, start by asking the team (or community or family) to describe what it looks like when they are operating at their best (the idea outcome in other words). Some questions can help here to guide that process. For example, for a team looking to operate well together:

- What does it feel like in that future state?

- How do people describe you as a team?

- When you go home at night, how do you feel about your team?

Capture these ideas using Post-It® notes, or on a digital whiteboard or 3x5 cards.

Then split the team up into groups and have them draw a simple picture of what success looks like in relationship to the challenge/objective.

INTUITION: Of all the things the group have captured, what seem to be the most salient points? Where are their common themes? Is there anything that everyone agrees on?

Now have everyone close their eyes and think about the team's success and which of these things will really help them move this forward.

Identify the top 20, then hone it to 10, then to 5.

1.

2.

3.

4.

5.

DESIRE: Which of these are the group drawn to? Once everyone has chosen the ideas that work best for them, take the time to look at what ideas are appealing to others.

Have everyone describe how it will make them feel when the outcome has been achieved or is integrated into your processes.

Ask questions like:

- Is this in alignment with who you are and what you are doing in the present moment?

- When you cast your net into the future what exciting things are you doing and being?

- What obstacles are you able to face?

In larger sessions you can do this in smaller groups and then have each team debrief to the larger group.

DRIVE: Now, either stay in the same teams or mix them up, then have each team take one of the ideas into the next part of the equation. With this idea:

- What small, immediate actions do we need to take to start to put this into place?

- Is there anything we are afraid of doing as we take action? Why?

- Who might we involve in this part of the process to get feedback, sponsor support, or gain alignment?

- List the big actions and break each one down into small action steps that are easier to take. Find 1–2 things your team can do right away.

Have each team present to the larger group and gain feedback.

Then calendar your actions and make time to meet again to course correct and measure your progress.

A FEW FINAL TIPS FOR GROUP SESSIONS

1. All ideas should be captured with Post-It® notes, drawings, models on the tables or objects. With dozens of ideas to choose from, now the team can hone them down to 1–2 to incubate/test in the real world. AND save the other load of ideas to go back to and germinate in the future.

2. A cool (NOT freezing!) room keeps everyone awake. One team asked someone to bring them bathrobes and they wore them over their clothes to stay warm. Subsequently they weren't lulled into sleep.

3. Competition between teams ups their Creative Genius by dialing up their "win" drive and adds to the pressure of a less than optimal time frame. Applying pressure to a team and then renegotiating with them should they actually need more time, empowers them at the same time as well as keeping to the task set. Most procrastinators do better under pressure. Research shows that if we are given five days to complete a project, we will wait until the fifth day

to do the task. Most of us will procrastinate until the last day and then come up with something awesome.

THE CREATIVE GENIUS EQUATION IN ACTION

In an offsite workshop for a major TV network, the team wanted to come up with new product ideas related to one of their long-running shows. This was a team who have been working on the product range for years and the group included the CEO. They needed to build on their expertise but get out of their old idea mindset.

We designed a **GAME-STORMING** session where random ideas were mashed together:

1. Think of all of your favorite objects from big brands or things that bring you joy and write each one on a separate 3x5 card. Now pass that to another table.

2. Next, think of the best experience you had that forced you out of your comfort zone and write each of those on a separate card.

3. You now have two stacks of cards. Pass them to the table next to you.

4. Your job is to take one card from each stack and, with these two things, make up a new world based on these two qualities and build it using props we've provided. Give this world a name, then imagine the kinds of toys and products the people living in this made-up world are using.

5. Now rotate round the room and see other worlds and hear their descriptions.

EACH TEAM THEN HAD TO TAKE WHAT THEY SAW AND DESIGN PRODUCTS THAT WOULD BE NECESSARY IN THAT NEW WORLD.

In addition, they had to be able to explain why that product was necessary. These ideas were then used to stimulate new products that the team would take into development and beta-test.

When I look back at this process, I realize we had designed structured and convoluted play! But their "play" required them to ask more questions, put weird things together and purposefully lob ideas over the wall to each other. All of this forced them to think differently.

The whole process set the stage for both their intuition and intellect to step forward and introduce key ideas to incubate. When they loved an idea, they'd get super excited about it.

THE IDEA OF TURNING WORK INTO PLAY AND FOCUS INTO FUN HELPED TO PRODUCE UNEXPECTED OUTCOMES. THEY LEVERAGED THEIR INNATE CREATIVE GENIUS TO GET TO MORE AND BETTER IDEAS.

THANK YOU!

There are so many, many, many people who have helped to shape this book and to each of you, named and unnamed, I give a ginormous hug filled with heartfelt gratitude.

First, thanks to my clients and **CREATIVE GENIUS YOU** students for your ideas, your support, your Creative Genius. I admit to secretly beta testing many of these materials on you — LOL! And your feedback let me know what should stick! Thanks in arrears!

For editing and writing, I start with you, **PATRICIA KRYITSI HOWELL**, who slogged through early drafts of the material — you, my friend, went above and beyond. Followed by **CATE CARUTH** from **CREATIVE WORDS** who is truly a content alchemist with rounds of revisions and even input on illustration ideas — thank you so much! Thanks **ESTER HARRIS** for copywriting assistance, yes, you were right ;-). Thanks to **JAMIE SALOFF** for the amazing layout and making me recreate the font again and again and…you are so easy to work with, super wow and big love.

To all my super pals and supporters that helped buoy me up during the writing process **SUNNI B, FRANK M, NANCY C, DAWN P, PETE & HANNAH COHEN, HANNAH L, ANN Z, LEIGH ANNE T-K, CYNDY S** & all the **DEBRUCE** peeps. Especially all of you amazing **DRAW YOUR FUTURE**® trained facilitators in the Creative Genius tribe, **CHAITRA V** and **WOMEN IN CLOUD, CAROL, JEFF** and **JAKE, JON, ROSA** and **DUKE**.

To **SCOTT WARD** the superstar illustrator and Mr. MacGyver best friend. Sorry I moved to Texas, it's a long way from the PNW. But that kitchen remodel brought us closer, right?! LOL! You are a gem and these illustrations rock!

Finally to my wife and life partner, **JULIE BOARDMAN**. You are a nut-ball and I thank you for listening to me go on and on and on about pretty much everything. You always step up with great ideas and some of them found their way into this book. ☺ My wish for you is that every car you ever wanted will magically manifest one at a time in the car port but in rotation so we have enough parking space. (P.S. Remember to make them hybrid ;-)

PATTI DOBROWOLSKI, author of **9 TIPS TO UP YOUR CREATIVE GENIUS** and **DRAWING SOLUTIONS: HOW VISUAL GOAL SETTING WILL CHANGE YOUR LIFE**, is founder of **UP YOUR CREATIVE GENIUS**, a consulting firm that uses visuals and creative processes to help companies and individuals around the world accelerate growth and change. A critically acclaimed comic performer, internationally recognized keynote speaker, writer and business consultant, she has brought innovative visual practices to Fortune 500 companies, NGOs and small businesses. She's a three-time TEDx speaker at TEDxRainier, "**DRAW YOUR FUTURE®**" and TEDxSacramento "**IMAGINATION CHANGES EVERYTHING**," and TEDxBend — **CREATIVE GENIUS: YOU.** Her large format visuals grace the walls of such clients as Microsoft, Nike, Starbucks, Pepsico, Samsung, The Bill & Melinda Gates Foundation and the Seattle Space Needle to name just a few.

Bellingham artist **SCOTT WARD** creates paintings that are vibrant, yet subtle; vital and contemplative, and full of the light-hearted spirit that bridges the gap between the surreal and sublime, with images that speak not only to the eyes, but to the heart, mind and spirit as well. His paintings are a reflection of life in its manifold guises. Through the use of people, animals and stunning landscapes, all characterized by bold color, careful attention to light and shadow, graceful lines and an often startling juxtaposition, each work is a self-portrait of self expression for the artist. **SCOTT HAS WORKED AS AN ARTIST AND DESIGNER** in advertising, clothing design, graphic design, theater design, landscape design, interior design and murals, and has shown work at many galleries around the country. Whether a painting, print or note card, every piece of Scott Ward's art is invested with his spirit, his soul, and his thought-provoking take on everyday life, yet still allows the outsider room in which to add their own meaning, depth and perception to the mix.

CPSIA information can be obtained
at www.ICGtesting.com
Printed in the USA
VHW091805050123
598BV00003B/2